52 Connecticut and Rhode Island Weekends

GREAT GETAWAYS AND ADVENTURES FOR EVERY SEASON

MICHAEL SCHUMAN

COUNTRY ROADS PRESS

NTC/Contemporary Publishing Group

Library of Congress Cataloging-in-Publication Data

Schuman, Michael A.
    52 Connecticut and Rhode Island Weekends / Michael A. Schuman.
        p.   cm.
    Includes index.
    ISBN 1-56626-183-X (paper)
      1. Connecticut—Guidebooks.   2. Rhode Island—Guidebooks.
  I. Title.
  F92.3.S37   1997
  917.4604′43—dc21   97-10052
                                                      CIP

Cover and interior design by Nick Panos
Cover and interior illustrations copyright © Jill Banashek
Map by Mapping Specialists, Madison, Wisconsin
Picture research by Elizabeth Broadrup Lieberman

Published by Country Roads Press
A division of NTC/Contemporary Publishing Group, Inc.
4255 West Touhy Avenue, Lincolnwood (Chicago), Illinois 60646-1975 U.S.A.
Copyright © 1999 by Michael Schuman
Printed in the United States of America
International Standard Book Number: 1-56626-183-X
99 00 01 02 03 04 QP 19 18 17 16 15 14 13 12 11 10 9 8 7 6 5 4 3 2 1

To Patti, Trisha, and Alexandra, and in memory of Kelila

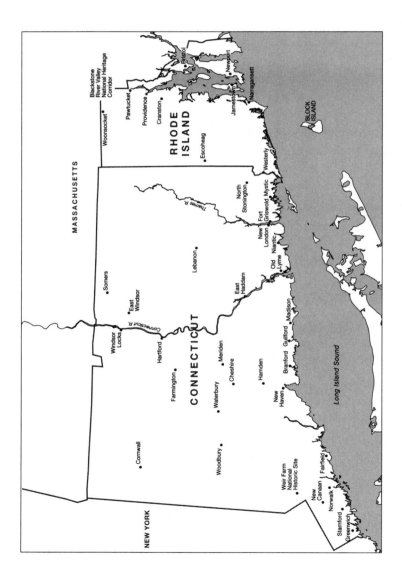

Contents

Fall

Winter

Introduction

IT'S ALL RELATIVE.

When you talk about southern New England, that three-word platitude is so true. If you live in New Jersey, you think Connecticut is New Hampshire. If you live in New Hampshire, you think Connecticut is New Jersey.

As for Rhode Island, that's the little flyspeck home to either leisure-class blue bloods or the New England Mafia, depending on what you read or whom you talk to.

Now for the truth.

I live in New Hampshire, but I grew up in West Hartford, Connecticut, right in the belly button of the Constitution State, so I have long been familiar with southern New England's cozy villages, lush countryside, waterways, urban centers, historic industrial towns, and saltwater beaches and the many excuses to throw a weekend-long festival.

I grew up knowing that Mark Twain wrote his best works in a city on the banks of a big river, but not the one in Hannibal, Missouri. When my family went to the beach, we went to Long Island Sound, not to Cape Cod or the Jersey shore. In fifth grade, the most anticipated day of spring was the class trip to Mystic Seaport. Years later, when I went to the ocean with my high school friends, we went to Misquamicut in Rhode Island, where the big waves are.

I always knew Newport was not only the place with the most glorious mansions this side of Versailles, but also the home of the Touro Synagogue, oldest in the United States. I knew Litchfield County was the place to go to see the fall colors; there are places there that look more like Vermont than parts of Vermont itself.

Yet, after growing up in New England and attending undergraduate college in upstate New York, I wanted out. I moved to Los Angeles. After four years in southern California, I wanted back. As Johnny Carson once said, "Los Angeles is the place where in the fall they take away the green plastic trees and bring in the brown plastic trees."

The coolness and colors of our autumns, the inner warmth and wonder of our winter, the renaissance that comes every spring, our languid days of summer—they lured me back. I brought my wife, Patti, a native Angelino, home with me. She has learned to appreciate our four seasons and our heritage. If we are not cross-country skiing or loafing at the shore, we are exploring villages that thrived when George III was in power, or scouting out storied towns that once churned out woolens and buttons.

And we go to new places and events that did not exist when I was growing up, back when Ike and JFK occupied the Oval Office. In Norwalk there is a marvelous maritime center that's part aquarium, part museum, and part massive theater. In my own hometown of West Hartford is one of the country's most comprehensive collections of political memorabilia, the Museum of American Political Life.

The folks in northern Rhode Island have connected with the National Park Service to preserve the legacy of the industrial revolution along the Blackstone River Valley National Heritage Corridor. Every year, the sounds and culinary tastes of Louisiana come to the little village of Escoheag, Rhode Island, near the Connecticut border, and every day the sounds and musical tastes of Las Vegas are not far away at Foxwoods and Mohegan Sun casinos.

Our diversity, as you can see, is great, and I planned this book with diversity in mind. Covered are all corners of Rhode Island and Connecticut, from Cornwall to Newport, from Pawtucket to Greenwich. Discussed are all sorts of topics, from museums of history, to the best places to see migrating birds, to where to dash through the snow on a one-horse open sleigh, to the homes of artists and authors.

Described are multi-event roundups and detailed looks at special distinations.

No attraction or event paid to be included. I have been covering New England as a travel writer since 1979, and I chose the subjects based on my own experiences. If I have been someplace and found it not worthy of a visit, it is not in the book.

However, there is no way I could possibly include every worthwhile event or attraction in Connecticut and Rhode Island. This book is meant to be a sampling, not a complete listing. My goal is to help people find ways to enjoy themselves while sampling southern New England's character. I would have had to write a tome the size of Webster's unabridged dictionary to sufficiently discuss every commendable sight, festival, and activity in the region.

That said, please remember that travel, like movies and food, is subjective. One person's fascinating exhibit is another person's ode to boredom. One person's fun event is another person's waste of time. But bear in mind that each place or event mentioned is reflective in some way of the flavor of southern New England, and should also be fun to visit.

Happy wanderings!

How to Use This Book

52 Connecticut and Rhode Island Weekends is organized by season, but many of the discussed trips are by no means limited to certain times of the year. It is simply neater to put indoor places in winter and outdoor destinations in summer. Then again, some trips naturally fit into categories. Fall festivals take place, of course, in fall. Spring blossoms come out in spring. Polar bears might venture to the ocean in January, but not many of the rest of us do. And you won't see The Breakers decked out in its Christmas best in July.

For weekend trips taking you to one attraction or one region, I offer lodging suggestions. I tried to list a mix of chain and independent motels, B and Bs and inns, and expensive and less expensive lodging. (Unfortunately, there is no such thing as inexpensive lodging in southern New England.) Bear in mind that a listing does not mean I am endorsing or recommending any place to stay. These are only suggestions.

Also, for some singular attractions, I added a listing called "When in the area," where I cite nearby places described elsewhere in the book. This is helpful if you want to combine a few destinations in one weekend trip.

I don't own stock in MCI or Sprint, but I suggest you use the phone, especially if you are making a special trip. Since hours and days open can change depending on budget and staffing, information listed in that category is fairly general. Similarly, I tried to mention which attractions are closed on which holidays, but this too can change. In fact, anything can change, so I urge you to call first rather than risk disappointment.

A note on safety: Our regional contribution to medical science is Lyme disease, discovered right here in Connecticut. It is caused by deer ticks which can be found just about anyplace outdoors. Before enjoying a leisurely amble in the woods, you might want to ask a staff person how prevalent the ticks are in that specific area.

Finally, if you would like additional information, please contact the following:

Connecticut Office of Tourism
505 Hudson Street
Hartford, CT 06106
(800) CT-BOUND (282-6863)
www.state.ct.us/tourism/

Rhode Island Tourism Division
1 West Exchange Street
Providence, RI 02903
(800) 556-2484 or (401) 222-2601;
www.visitrhodeisland.com

Spring

1

A Bounty of Blossoms

IN 1936, FRANKLIN ROOSEVELT'S NEW DEAL WAS IN FULL swing, Margaret Mitchell published *Gone with the Wind*, and the National Baseball Hall of Fame was established in Cooperstown, New York. In May of that year in the homey Greenfield Hill section of Fairfield, Connecticut, some local women set up a card table in front of the Greenfield Hill Congregational Church, where they sold crafts and canned pickles.

Sales were good. After all, they had a ready-made clientele. The white and pink dogwood blossoms of Greenfield Hill were in full bloom, and the women knew that in May people came in hordes to see the blossoms the same way travelers head north to New Hampshire and Vermont to admire the autumn leaves.

The women sold more crafts and pickles the next year and more the year after that. As demand increased, they added cookies, punch, and sandwiches to their stock. Before long, their impromptu sale in front of the church had turned into a full-fledged festival.

Nowadays the Greenfield Hill Congregational Church's Dogwood Festival is one of Connecticut's biggest events. There are more than 30,000 dogwoods in the Greenfield Hill section of Fairfield, and they continue to show off their white and pink blossoms for visitors. According to one staffer, the roads boasting the best blooms are Congress

Street, Bronson Road, and Old Academy Road, on which the church is located.

The festival is more than a floral feast. Crafts are sold and sometimes demonstrated; weavers, blacksmiths, and wood turners are common. Paintings and plants are sold, and kids can make tissue flowers or watch artists take paintbrushes to their faces.

Visitors can also appreciate Fairfield's long colonial heritage. Guided walking tours into private backyards and gardens show the Early American side of one of the country's most famous suburbs. To add atmosphere, guides don colonial costumes. The tour's highlight might be the English garden behind the historic Varick Day House. It looks just as an English garden should look, with a boxwood hedge symmetrically surrounding statuary, lawn paths, and fountains. It was designed by Frederick Law Olmstead, America's landscape architect extraordinaire of the 19th century.

The Dogwood Festival begins the Saturday before Mother's Day and lasts five days.

Two other towns in Connecticut flaunt their blossoms with spring festivals. In 1970 a resident of Hamden and native of Portugal named Chris Rendeiro joined forces with then Mayor William Adams to create the Goldenbells Festival. Rendeiro remembered the community celebrations common in Portugal and felt Hamden should have one of its own.

Hamden is home to acres of goldenbells, also known as forsythia, which show off their yellow blossoms in late April and early May. So, it was decided to make the goldenbells the theme of Hamden's special event.

This flower fest lasts about three weeks and there are numerous events, many unrelated to goldenbells or gardening. Those that are related include the blessing of the goldenbells at Saint Joan of Arc Church (a Catholic service followed by the nondenominational blessing), a spring wild-flower hike in Sleeping Giant State Park, and talks and demonstrations on caring for and arranging flowers and plants. Cruise Shepard Street for the best views of goldenbells in bloom.

In Meriden, daffodils are extolled. A bumper sticker distributed to celebrants at the weekend-long Daffodil Festival reads, "577,315 Daffodils Can't Be Wrong."

Hubbard Park is the setting of the late-April event and also the best place to see daffodils in bloom. You might also see human-size daffodils in Saturday's parade. One recent float featured little kids dressed as the yellow flowers standing in a field. Another, sponsored by an area hairstyling salon, had models wearing hairdos resembling avant-garde daffodils.

Other events include a juried craft fair, Saturday-night fireworks, and the "Silver Fork" tent with ethnic foods representing Meriden's cultural diversity.

FOR MORE INFORMATION

Location: Fairfield
Contact: Dogwood Chairman, Greenfield Hill Congregational Church, 1045 Old Academy Road, Fairfield, CT 06430; (203) 259 5596.
Lodging: Fairfield Motor Inn, 417 Post Road, Fairfield, CT; (800) 257-0496 or (203) 255-0491. Bridgeport Holiday Inn, 1070 Main Street, Bridgeport, CT; (203) 334-1234.

Location: Hamden
Contact: Kaye Hammond, 220 Garvin Road, Hamden, CT 06518; (203) 281-4768.
Lodging: Days Inn, 3400 Whitney Avenue, Hamden, CT; (203) 288-2505. Howard Johnson Lodge, 2260 Whitney Avenue, Hamden, CT; (203) 288-3831.

Location: Meriden

Contact: Parks and Recreation Department, 460 Liberty Street, Meriden, CT 06450; (203) 630-4259.

Lodging: Meriden Inn (a motel), 1102 East Main Street, Meriden, CT; (203) 634-4700. Hampton Inn, 10 Bee Street, Meriden, CT; (203) 235-5154.

2

Over and Under the Sea

THE BANKS OF THE THAMES (PRONOUNCE THE "TH" AND SAY it as if it rhymes with "games" and you won't sound like a tourist) River in southeastern Connecticut is where boats and sailors are made. The Electric Boat Division of General Dynamics in Groton, on the east side of the Thames, is the largest builder of submarines in the United States. Its most prized baby, USS *Nautilus*, is back home after logging tons and tons of miles across the globe, and you can tread the same scanty hallways that the cream of America's navy once hurried across.

On the west side of the Thames in New London is the U.S. Coast Guard Academy, one of four military academies in the country and the place where cadets learn everything from the intricacies of naval architecture and marine engineering to swabbing the deck.

A visit to both the USS *Nautilus* Memorial and the adjacent museum along with the Coast Guard Academy can make for a full day of exploring the art of seafaring on the southeast Connecticut coast.

The USS *Nautilus* Memorial is really two attractions in one. There is the first nuclear-powered sub, which was also the first to cruise under the geographic North Pole, accomplished in 1958. On the grounds is the Submarine Force Library and Museum, where the folklore and the realities of life in a floating undersea tin can are examined.

Those with an understanding of such things can study the mechanics of sonar operations or the wall of instruments used to designate the sub's direction and speed. Less technical types might wander through the narrow corridors of *Nautilus* and wonder how 116 men could stand living in such a closed-in space, replete with ever-present pungent smells of cooking, sweat, and tobacco.

Inside the museum are scale models of a diving bell and a World War II sub. There is also a periscope you can peer through to find your car in the parking lot.

On the other side of the Thames are the halls of the U.S. Coast Guard Academy, where the men and women who guard the seas receive their training. Visitor activities on the campus consist of three obligatory stops: the visitor center, the academy museum, and the barque *Eagle*.

The visitor center is a promotional valentine to the academy, but it is also the place to learn what it takes to become one of the 900 cadets here. One hears that the Coast Guard is the only armed service with a peacetime mission, which includes tracking icebergs, protecting ports and fisheries, and conducting search-and-rescue missions. An audio guide narrated by cadets can be borrowed at no cost, but the most eye-catching display might be the model of a Coast Guard ship, complete with resident helicopter and made from 20,002 Legos.

Across campus in Waesche Hall is the U.S. Coast Guard Museum, which is basically the Coast Guard's attic. Your view upon entering the huge hall that comprises the museum is dominated by a thirteen-foot-tall lighthouse lens, originally used in a lighthouse on Cape Anne in Massachusetts.

Wander around and you will see other nautical treasures. Linking the past to the present are pieces of the massive chain stretched across the Hudson River which cut the British fleet off from their army during the Revolutionary War. Life preservers from the doomed *Andrea Doria*, Civil

War-era cannons, ship models and paintings, and a plaque to a Coast Guard chief dog named Sinbad are additional relics.

To see the country's only active-duty square-rigger and the largest tall ship flying the American flag you have to step outside. Berthed on the Thames is *Eagle*, 147 feet at its highest point, 295 feet long, and a seagoing classroom for cadets. Our four-year-old thought *Eagle* sounded more like the name of an airplane than a boat, but it has a lengthy heritage. This is the seventh *Eagle*; the first was commissioned in 1792.

Eagle is a residence for officers and enlisted personnel, so you likely will not be permitted to enter the living quarters. But there is much to see on the decks, including more than 22,000 square feet of sail and five miles of rigging. Kids have fun pretending to be captain at the big ship's wheels.

For More Information

Location: The U.S. Coast Guard Academy is located off Route 32 in New London. From Interstate 95, heading north take exit 82A, heading south take exit 83.

Admission: No charge.

Hours: The Coast Guard Academy is open daily. We urge you to call in advance if you have your heart set on seeing the tall ship, *Eagle*, which can be on the water or in use for training at any time. Visitors on Fridays in April, May, September, or October have an excellent chance of seeing a Corps of Cadets Review on Washington Parade Ground at 4 P.M. In summer both the cadets and *Eagle* are away. In winter *Eagle* is in dry dock in Maryland.

Contact: U.S. Coast Guard Academy, 15 Mohegan Avenue, New London, CT 06320-4195; (860) 444-8611 (visitor center), (860) 444-8511 (museum), or (860) 444-8595 (*Eagle*).

Over and Under the Sea

Location: USS *Nautilus* and the Submarine Force Library and Museum are on Route 12. Take Interstate 95, exit 6, and head north to the site.

Admission: No charge.

Hours: Daily in late spring, summer, and early fall; closed Tuesday the rest of the year. The site also closes for one week in both May and December for maintenance.

Contact: *Nautilus* Memorial, Box 571, Naval Submarine Base New London, Groton, CT 06349-5000. Visitors are asked to call (800) 343-0079 or (860) 449-3174 for recorded basic information. For answers to specific questions, call (860) 449-3558.

When in the area: Mystic, a short drive east, is home to Mystic Seaport (Chapter 12) and the Mystic Marinelife Aquarium (Chapter 43). In Groton is Fort Griswold State Park with its battle monument commemorating Connecticut's claim to Revolutionary War fame (Chapter 38).

Lodging: Quality Inn, 404 Bridge Street, Groton, CT; (860) 445-8141. Groton Inn & Suites, 99 Gold Star Highway (Route 184), Groton, CT; (800) 452-2191 or (860) 445-9784. Red Roof Inn, 707 Colman Street, New London, CT; (860) 444-0001. Queen Anne Inn (a Victorian inn with antique furnishings), 265 Williams Street, New London, CT; (800) 347-8818 or (860) 447-2600.

3

Newport's Mansions in Spring

PHILANTHROPIST AND RAILROAD HEIR CORNELIUS VANDER-
bilt II was said to break into a grin about as frequently as the
Cubs win the pennant. Ironic, isn't it, that he is responsible
for probably the most lavish mansion of the many open to
the public in the Gilded Age resort town of Newport, Rhode
Island.

His palace (excuse me, "summer cottage"), The Breakers,
boasts vaulted ceilings with gilt-framed oil-on-canvas paintings, Baccarat crystal chandeliers, rare marble mantels, and
a dining room that would be perfectly at home in Louis XIV's
Versailles.

In summer, it also has crowds—elbowing, obtrusive,
annoying, waiting—as do the other famous Newport mansions: Marble House, Rosecliff, Belcourt Castle, Chateau Sur
Mer, The Elms, Beechwood, and all the rest. Which is one
main reason why the Preservation Society of Newport
County, administrator of most of the Newport mansions,
recommends a springtime weekend.

Lines in spring are as rare as blizzards. Tours are more
relaxed, and visitors receive increased individual attention.
Guides can answer questions or chat with visitors without
concern about the next horde on its way in.

The same holds true for restaurants. During July and
August, two-hour waits for tables are common.

But in spring, there is also a difference in what you see.
Azaleas, laurel, rhododendrons, and cherry trees show off all

over the city. The pear trees at The Breakers are at their showiest.

The Breakers, though, is just one of Newport's Gilded Age gems. On Bellevue Avenue is a parade of palaces. Just to the south of The Breakers is Marble House, the summer residence of Cornelius's brother, William Kissam Vanderbilt, a leisure-loving man who spent his spare time and money on parties, polo, and taking yacht to water. He also had $11 million which he invested in the building of Marble House in 1892. Of that total, $7 million was spent on imported marble.

Farther up Bellevue Avenue is the Astors' Beechwood, the only mansion with a living-history guided tour. Enter the doors of Beechwood and the year is 1891. The guides are frozen in the characters of Mrs. Caroline Astor's distinguished guests and domestic workers, telling their tales of life living with or working for the rich and famous in Gilded Age Newport. Beechwood is significantly less ostentatious than the two Vanderbilt mansions.

There are several other mansions open to the public. The list includes: Rosecliff and The Elms, both built in the early 1900s; Belcourt Castle, constructed in 1891; a mid-Victorian-era marvel, Chateau Sur Mer, built in 1852; and Kingscote, an 1839 masterpiece.

There is one drawback to a spring visit. Don't expect a relaxing swim as a break from sight-seeing. Newport isn't Miami, and people aren't penguins. But the beaches still lure, as does the famed Cliff Walk which parallels the Atlantic. Spring walks along either are as relaxing as in the summer. The only difference is that you will likely wear long pants.

For More Information

Location: The majority of mansions are on or just off Bellevue Avenue.

Admission: There is a charge to view all mansions.

Hours: Most mansions are open for the season on weekends in April, and daily in May. Most close at the end of October but reopen for the holiday season as part of the Christmas in Newport celebration (Chapter 48). The majority stay closed the rest of winter. An exception is Belcourt Castle, which is open year-round.

Contact: The Astors' Beechwood, (401) 846-3772. Belcourt Castle, (401) 846-0669. Breakers, Marble House, Rosecliff, The Elms, Chateau Sur Mer, and Kingscote, (401) 847-1000.

When in the area: Hunter House (Chapter 37), the International Tennis Hall of Fame (Chapter 19), and the Naval War College Museum (Chapter 15) are a few of the other Newport attractions open in spring.

Lodging: This is the B and B capital of southern New England. A partial list of Newport B and Bs includes: Cliffside Inn (former home of artist Beatrice Turner and repository for many of her works), 2 Seaview Avenue; (800) 845-1811 or (401) 847-1811. The Wayside, 406 Bellevue Avenue; (401) 847-0302. The Jailhouse Inn (a restored colonial jail), 13 Marlborough Street; (401) 847-4638. Brinley Victorian Inn, 23 Brinley Street; (800) 999-8523 or (401) 849-7645. The Willows, 8-10 Willow Street; (401) 846-5486.

There is also a B and B service listing rooms in more than 150 private homes, inns, and guest houses: Anna's Victorian Connection, 5 Fowler Avenue, Newport, RI 02840; (800) 884-4288 or (401) 849-2489.

Conventional motels in Newport include: Motel 6, 249 J. T. Connell Highway; (401) 848-0600. Best Western Mainstay Inn, 151 Admiral Kalbfus Road; (401) 849-9880. Newport Harbor Hotel & Marina, 49 America's Cup Avenue; (401) 847-9000.

Newport's Mansions in Spring

4

Maple Sugar Time

ACTUALLY IT'S SAP, A WATERY FLUID WITH A LOW SUGAR content, that flows from the maples. One maple farmer said, "You would be surprised to find out how many people think syrup flows directly from trees."

In early spring when daytime temperatures rise above freezing but nights are still cold, the sap begins to run up the tree from its root system. The trees are tapped and the sap flows into either galvanized buckets (the old-fashioned way) or clear plastic tubing (the modern way). Buckets of sap have to be gathered by hand, while with tubing the sap flows directly into the sugarhouse. Ultimately, the sap is placed inside a tank called an evaporator and is boiled continuously until the water is removed. Pure maple syrup is the result, and it generally takes thirty to forty gallons of sap to make one gallon of syrup.

One premier early-spring event in southern New England is the Maple Sugaring Festival at the Inn on Lake Waramaug in New Preston. To paraphrase one long-ago big band leader, become a professor in the college of sugaring knowledge as you observe demonstrations of the tedium involved in turning sap into syrup.

Those picturesque galvanized steel buckets that for so long were used for collecting sap from trees have been replaced among progress-minded farmers by plastic tubing connecting the inn's maples. Area maple farmers explain the intricacies of exactly how the tubing works. Young people wanting to try their hand at tapping trees the old-fashioned way can do so with maple stumps brought specifically for the event. They can then relax on a hayride across the inn grounds.

What about food? There are waffles, ice cream covered with maple syrup, maple candies, jellies, and sugar on snow, that peculiar New England treat of syrup thickened to a caramel-like texture and poured over snow or crushed ice. It's often topped with a pickle to offset the sweetness and is not part of any certified weight-loss plan. Inn on Lake Waramaug, 107 North Shore Road, New Preston, CT 06777; (800) LAKE-INN (525-3466) or (203) 868-0563.

Sugarhouses and Syrup Centers

Since 1966 the Flanders Nature Center in Woodbury has been making syrup at its sugarhouse on Cowles Road. It is open for tours and demonstrations on most weekend afternoons in March, and volunteers are welcome to lend a hand collecting sap, preparing firewood for the furnace, or packaging syrup. The center even publishes a small booklet with recipes and instructions for those wishing to tap trees in their backyards and make maple syrup in the comfort of their own homes. Flanders Nature Center, PO Box 702, Woodbury, CT 06798-0702; (203) 263-3711.

Who says you have to go to Vermont or New Hampshire to visit an old-fashioned family-run sugarhouse? There are several spread across Connecticut. Most of the following offer samples and sell syrup by the container. You might also be able to buy maple candies and maple butter. Before making a spontaneous visit to any of these sites, keep in mind that the availability of maple syrup, like any other agricultural product, depends on the whims of nature. Sugaring season can change from one year to the next. If you want to be certain to see the sugaring process in all its glory, we urge you to call ahead.

FOR MORE INFORMATION

Lamothe's Sugar House: Located at 89 Stone Road, RFD #3, Burlington, CT 06013; (203) 675-5043. Guided tours last approximately twenty-five minutes. Demonstrations of tree tapping and modern tubing are given. Sugar on snow is served on request, and baby animals such as piglets, kittens, puppies, and rabbits are on hand for entertainment.

Rock House Maple Syrup: Located at 150 Rock House Road, Easton, CT 06612; (203) 268-0059. A self-guided tour both outdoors and indoors helps you explore the sugaring process. Come at the right time and you might see maple candies being made.

Kasulaitis Farm and Sugarhouse: Located at 69 Goose Green Road, New Hartford, CT 06057; (203) 379-8787. The informal tour here lets you observe the sugaring process as well as learn about the history of maple-syrup making.

Wayne's Sugarhouse: Located at 89 Cedar Lake Road, North Branford, CT 06471; (203) 488-3549. The tour here is mostly inside the sugarhouse. You can also see gallons of sap being delivered by truck from the woods.

Sweet Sue's Sugar Shack: Sweet Sue is Sue Langer, who with husband Doug operates this Windham County farm. The guided tour takes you from the buckets hanging in the yard to the wood-fired evaporator indoors.

Norman's Sugarhouse: Located at 387 County Road, Woodstock, CT 06281; (203) 974-1235. Watch sap being made into syrup in two wood-fired evaporators in the Norman family's sugarhouse. Those tending the fire will explain the process and answer questions.

Maple Sugar Time

5

Craft Shop Till You Drop

AT THE EASTERN END OF BRANFORD NEAR THE GUILFORD town line is a shopping center that's not your usual shopping center. Bittersweet Farm consists of nine rustic and handsome buildings, once part of a chicken farm on Route 1.

There are still chickens here, but they can be seen only in the rear of the property, along with turkeys, goats, and other animals, walking and squawking and craving attention. Tucked amid the beams in the elongated building known as The Marketplace you will likely find birds' nests, especially in the spring or early summer. Birds find the place hospitable and seem to return each year to build homes.

The shopkeepers are no less cordial. As a woodworker sat carving a mahogany dolphin, we chatted about everything from the texture of different woods to some no-good bum the New York Yankees just acquired. While we admired handsome wooden Christmas ornaments in the shapes of lobsters, fish, and crabs, the carver joked about their diminutive size. "When my brain goes dead at the end of the day, that's when I make those small things," he said.

In another building, a glassblower explained that the temperature in his oven was about 2,000 degrees. "Just part of the job," he said. In another shop, we admired an array of quilts, some with patterns of dinosaurs and cats, sure to rivet the attention of even a restless four-year-old.

Upstairs in The Marketplace building are artists' studios, where you can watch craftspersons create the same works they sell. This includes handmade stained glass, dolls, hand-knits, and the intricate, swirling paper-cuttings of Martha Walsh, former math teacher and one of the center's managers. Walsh's most popular items are sailboats, cats, and floral scenes.

Walsh was one of the earliest artisans to set up shop here, renting space in a former chicken coop in 1972. Actually, it was in the 1960s that former Bittersweet Farm owner Robert Wallace first began renting space to craftspersons. One version of the story says that Wallace noticed that small farms were turning up in the also-ran category when competing with huge poultry companies, so he decided to convert chicken coops to studios.

Another, says Martha Walsh, is that "Bob Wallace was a free spirit who wanted this to be an artists' colony, with or without chickens. Some say he was born at the wrong place at the wrong time, he should have been an artist."

When Walsh first came, she was one of four craftspersons, along with a jeweler, an upholsterer, and a potter. The early days, she says, were "very quiet, except for the chickens."

The conversion from chicken farm to craft colony was completed in 1977. Wallace died in 1982, and the property was sold, but the new owners continued to keep the chicken farm as a place where crafts, not eggs, are the products for sale.

Round out a craft-shopping visit to southern Connecticut by heading a few miles east to historic Guilford, home of the Guilford Handcraft Center. Founded in 1962, this establishment is a combination arts-and-crafts school, gallery showcase, and shop where more than four hundred American artisans are represented.

You will find jewelry, basketry, pottery, clothing, and metalwork for sale. Specifically, you might run across anything from a burled-wood decorative box, to a blown-glass perfume bottle, to earrings in the shape of cats, to men's ties and children's toys.

Want to learn to make your own craft work? The Guilford center holds classes for every age group. While you are picking up the fine techniques of malachite or tortoise-shell painting, your kindergartener can be discovering methods of making a papier-mâché horse or a terra-cotta clay box.

Both the Branford and Guilford craft centers host major shows. Branford's are in early July and October. Guilford Handcraft Exposition, their biggest event, is in mid-July, with a holiday craft festival in November and December.

For More Information

Location: Branford Craft Center is located on Route 1 (East Main Street) in town. The Guilford Handcraft Center is on Route 77 (Church Street).

Admission: No charge.

Hours: Branford Craft Center is open Tuesday through Saturday, and Sunday afternoon. Some artists' studios might be closed on Sunday. Guilford's craft shop is open Monday through Saturday, and Sunday afternoon.

Contact: Branford Craft Village at Bittersweet Farm, 779 East Main Street, Branford, CT 06405; (203) 488-4689. Guilford Handcraft Center, Inc., PO Box 589, 411 Church Street, Guilford, CT 06437; (203) 453-5947.

When in the area: To see more objects of art, though not necessarily for sale, visit the museums of Yale University to the west (Chapter 46), or the small museums of the former Old Lyme art colony, about a half hour east (Chapter 28).

Lodging: Motel 6, 320 East Main Street (Route 1), Branford, CT; (203) 483-5828. MacDonald's Motel, 565 East Main Street (Route 1), Branford, CT; (203) 488-4381. Guilford Suites Hotel, 2300 Boston Post Road (Route 1), Guilford, CT; (203) 453-0123. Tower Motel, 320 Boston Post Road (Route 1), Guilford, CT; (203) 453-9069.

Craft Shop Till You Drop

6

Daffodils, Gargoyles, Chickens, and Hops

THE VIEW OF SEAGULLS GLIDING OVER NARRAGANSETT BAY from Blithewold's outdoor loggia can't help but make one think of the upcoming summer months. But the close-at-hand view of more than 50,000 daffodils in resplendent bloom in Blithewold's gardens says spring all over.

Meanwhile, down on the farm—the Coggeshall Farm Museum—the oxen are pulling a plow, getting fields in shape for 1790s-style planting in this re-created colonial Rhode Island farm.

A visit to Blithewold Mansion & Gardens is a double-treat—a late-Gilded Age anything-but-humble home and a combination arboretum and gardens that could stand on their own as a welcoming park.

The name "Blithewold" means "happy woodland" in Middle English, and one can spend his or her time happily examining original Tiffany furnishings inside the mansion or the largest giant sequoia east of the Rockies in the thick of the arboretum. Or you can relax and joke around, waiting for your tour to start, as did a father with four children on our tour. As we sat on the loggia, the father described how each of the four carved gargoyles over the big glass doors resembled his four children.

"No," protested a boy about ten. "That monkey gargoyle looks more like Sara."

Wisecracks aside, Blithewold is a serious charmer. It was completed as a summer home in 1908 for owners William and Bessie Van Winkle McKee. Bessie originally moved to this spot in 1896 with Augustus Van Winkle, a Pennsylvania coal-mining magnate. Augustus had only two years to enjoy the original 1896 wooden clapboard mansion before dying in a hunting accident in 1898. The original home burned to the ground eight years later; the stone-and-stucco mansion you see today is its 1908 replacement.

Incorporated into the design of the new mansion was the sweeping view of Narragansett Bay. One can see the bay from every room. But it is just as easy to be distracted by the interior furnishings—the Russian samovar, the Middle Eastern beverage cooler (looking like a refugee from an "Aladdin" movie), the bed box from Brittany, and the Swedish music box, all brought back by their owners while on world travels.

Although this was a summer home only, Gilded Age formality never placed second to comfort. We heard in the English dining room how for nightly dinner men dressed in tuxedos and women dressed in formal gowns, regardless of how hot and humid the weather was. Consider that this was decades before air-conditioning and the use of deodorants became commonplace. Yuck.

Bessie was an accomplished horticulturist, and the fruits of her passion cover the grounds. Most of the trees and shrubs are native to Japan, China, and Korea and date to the early 1900s. Some of their appearances are sure to spark a smile, even among the most uninterested brown thumb. The leaves on the ginkgo tree resemble little fans. Those on the ketsura tree are in the shape of valentines a child might draw. In the bamboo grove, one woman on our tour commented that the plants look like a field of fishing poles stacked side by side.

In spring the daffodils make the biggest splash, but the crocuses and scylla blossom first, in early April. The flowering cherry in the water garden comes out in late April, and the tulips blossom usually in early May. June is the month for roses, but you will see something in bloom in any warm-weather month.

Blithewold hosts concerts in summer and decks out in its best holiday attire for Christmas. See Chapters 18 and 49.

To round out a visit and to amuse restless youngsters, take a ten-minute drive through the eye-pleasing town of Bristol to Coggeshall Farm. Here children can watch sheep, pigs, oxen, chickens, and cows while adults will have the benefit of knowing that they are seeing rare breeds in action. Those on the farm are similar to the breeds found on any Rhode Island farm in the 1790s.

In spring, costumed staff members plow fields and plant seeds for crops such as asparagus, squash, corn, rye, hops, peas, and a variety of herbs. Visitors are encouraged to lend a hand, whether it means taking a shot at milking a cow or grabbing a bucket of feed at animal dinnertime.

For More Information

Location: Blithewold Mansion & Gardens is on Route 114 (Ferry Road), south of the center of Bristol. Coggeshall Farm Museum is adjacent to Colt Park. From Route 114, north of the center of Bristol, turn left onto Poppasquash Road and follow 1.2 miles to the farm entrance. (You will pass an entrance to Colt Park—ignore it.)

Admission: A fee is charged for both sites.

Hours: The grounds at Blithewold are open year-round, daily. Mansion tours are offered April through October, Tuesday through Sunday. House and garden admission $8, $5 for garden only. Coggeshall Farm is open year-round, daily.

Contact: Blithewold Mansion & Gardens, 101 Ferry Road, Bristol, RI 02809-0716; (401) 253-2707. Coggeshall Farm

Daffodils, Gargoyles, Chickens, and Hops

Museum, Inc., PO Box 562, Bristol, RI 02809; (401) 253-9062.

When in the area: Spectacular mansions (Chapter 3), museums devoted to tennis (Chapter 19) and yachting (Chapter 15), and the vestiges of a colonial seaport are just down the road in Newport.

Lodging: Ramada Inn & Conference Center, 144 Anthony Road (junction of Routes 24 and 138), Portsmouth, RI; (401) 683-3600. Founder's Brook Motel & Suites, 314 Boyd's Lane, (junction of Routes 24 and 138), Portsmouth, RI; (401) 683-1244. Joseph Reynolds House Inn (a B and B), 956 Hope Street, Bristol, RI; (800) 754-0230 or (401) 254-0230. Rockwell House Inn B and B, 610 Hope Street, Bristol, RI; (800) 815-0040 or (401) 253-0040.

Spring

7

Colonial Hartford

PEOPLE FAMILIAR WITH STATEHOUSES IN BOSTON AND Augusta, Maine, might find themselves making comparisons before they even set foot inside Hartford's 1796 Old State House. All three buildings were designed by Charles Bulfinch, the same man who planned Boston's Faneuil Hall and was architect of the United States Capitol from 1818 to 1830.

The Old State House should be the first stop for anyone inspecting Hartford's long colonial heritage. It reopened in May 1996, its 200th birthday, after a four-year, $12 million renovation.

Those recalling the statehouse as an impressive but empty shell of a building will be astonished to see the activity buzzing around it today. Guides dress as colonial troops, merchants, or just plain citizens of the late 18th century. Twice a day as the building opens and closes, guards fire an exact replica of a 1780 cannon, and a farmers market takes place on weekdays in the late morning and early afternoon, reminiscent of the days when Meeting House Square was Hartford's town common.

Changes aside, the Old State House holds some impressive distinctions. It is the oldest statehouse in the country built specifically to house state government. It was Bulfinch's first public commission. And it was the first public building built of both brick and brownstone.

Old State House officials proudly point out that it is one of the few buildings in the United States displaying a Gilbert Stuart portrait of George Washington hanging where it was originally meant to hang. The portrait is one of only four full-length ones Stuart painted of Washington, and it hangs bordered by velvet and gold-festooned drapery above the three officers' chairs in the Senate chamber.

The Senate, or Governor's Council as it was initially called, first met here on May 13, 1796, and the Senate room has been restored to its appearance of two centuries ago. A total of twenty senators' chairs are original. You will need an expert to tell the originals from the mid-20th-century reproductions. Old Connecticut law books sit opened on tables, as do reproduced wooden ballot boxes.

Elsewhere in the city is the Connecticut Historical Society's museum at its Elizabeth Street headquarters. Heavy on decorative arts, the historical society museum showcases artifacts such as Bible boxes, tall clocks, and rows and rows of antique furniture. The two newest displays, added in 1998, are a multi-media exhibit devoted to the uprising on the slave ship *Amistad*, immortalized in the 1998 film by the same name, and a hands-on gallery created just for kids. Youngsters can try dressing in clothes popular in past centuries, building a brick wall, or taking in the scents of boiling maple syrup and a steam locomotive.

And what does a bottle of Paul Newman salad dressing have to do with chunks of the renowned (to Connecticut residents, anyway) Charter Oak? They are among the tons of other objects in the society's collection, all having something to do with the heritage or commerce of the state. To display as much as possible, temporary exhibits show off everything from Connecticut-made bicycles to footwear.

Tucked in amid the glass and concrete of downtown Hartford is the parklike Ancient Burying Ground. Adjacent to the 1807 Center Church Meeting House at 60 Gold Street, the cemetery contains a gravestone dating to 1663. Its most famous resident is Thomas Hooker, regarded as the founder of Connecticut. Tradition says Hooker is buried under the church which has a memorial plaque to him on its west wall.

Others buried here may not have been famous but were as complex and diverse personalities as people living in any other time. Look for the marker of Lieutenant William Knox, who ran a tavern near the town ferry, where he housed British prisoners of war during the American Revolution. His epitaph, part admonition, part tart taunt, and common to several gravestones in New England, reads:

> *"Behold my friend as you pass by.*
> *As you are now so once was I;*
> *As I am now, so you must be.*
> *Prepare for death and follow me."*

For More Information

Location: The Old State House is at 800 Main Street, downtown. From Interstate 91, take exit 31; from Interstate 84, take exit 52. Connecticut Historical Society is at 1 Elizabeth Street, near the junction with Asylum Avenue. From Interstate 84, take exit 46 onto West Boulevard; turn right on Whitney Street, then right onto Elizabeth Street. The Ancient Burying Ground is at 60 Gold Street, downtown.
Admission: The Old State House and Ancient Burying Ground are free; admission is charged for the Connecticut Historical Society, except for the first Sunday of the month.
Hours: The Old State House is open Monday through Saturday, and Sunday afternoon. The Connecticut Historical Society museum is open Tuesday through Sunday, afternoons only (closed Saturday in summer and on major holi-

days). The Ancient Burying Ground is open daily, dawn to dusk. Church tours are given by appointment. **Contact:** Old State House, 800 Main Street, Hartford, CT; (860) 522-6766. The Connecticut Historical Society, 1 Elizabeth Street, Hartford, CT 06105; (860) 236-5621. Ancient Burying Ground Association, PO Box 31257, Hartford, CT 06103; (860) 249-5631.

When in the area: The homes of two of America's legendary authors, Mark Twain and Harriet Beecher Stowe, sit side by side and each can be explored (Chapter 47).

Lodging: Ramada Inn–Capitol Hill, 440 Asylum Street, Hartford, CT; (860) 246-6591. Super 8 Motel, 57 West Service Road, Hartford, CT; (860) 246-8888. Goodwin Hotel, 1 Haynes Street (across from the Civic Center), Hartford, CT; (800) 922-5006 or (860) 246-7500. The 1895 House B and B, 97 Girard Avenue, Hartford, CT; (860) 232-0014.

8

May Breakfasts

IN RHODE ISLAND THERE MAY BE NO GREATER STATEWIDE tradition than the May breakfast. In mid-spring, Rhode Islanders can be seen gathered in multitudes on early mornings and feasting on eggs, bacon, pancakes, johnnycakes, clam cakes, coffee cakes, corn bread, French toast, Danish, home fries, baked beans, apple pie, grits, bagels, doughnuts, muffins, and more. And for dessert . . .

The more than three dozen May breakfasts take place throughout the state from mid-April through early May. (Like Germany's Oktoberfest, which often begins in September, the feast's name doesn't necessarily represent its timetable.) Breakfasts are served mostly at churches but also in schools, fire stations, historical societies, and even a yacht club and a bird sanctuary.

And they are a long-standing tradition. When the first May breakfast was held, the American South was under occupation by Northern troops. It was 1867, and the Oak Lawn Community Baptist Church in the Oak Lawn district of Cranston served scrambled eggs, ham, corn bread, clam cakes, apple pie, coffee, tea, and milk. To this day, the same menu is served by waitresses in colonial Quaker costumes.

The second oldest is served at Park Place Congregational Church in Pawtucket. The parishioners there offered their first May breakfast in 1882.

Great-great-grandchildren of those who dished out eggs and pancakes way back when serve today at some long-standing May breakfasts, especially those at churches. Some breakfasts contain other legacies, such as food. The johnnycakes sold at the First Baptist Church of Kingstown's breakfast are made only from Kenyon's 1886 Grist Mill cornmeal. To true Rhode Islanders, real johnnycakes are made from locally grown and milled whitecap flint corn. Look around and you can find johnnycakes at other May breakfasts, too. But as the saying goes, caveat emptor.

The actual reason for the matutinal repasts dates to 1776. On May 4 of that fabled year, Rhode Island became the first colony to declare its independence from the Crown, something the other twelve colonies wouldn't do for two months. Because of Rhode Island's foresightedness, May became known as Heritage Month and became a cause for celebration.

And at most breakfasts nowadays you will find more for sale than clamcakes, eggs, and French toast. The scent of spring blossoms wafts through the air as flowers and May baskets deck dining rooms. Many of the floral offerings are sold in May baskets, which might also be filled with homemade fudge, cookies or other goodies. Craft sales are frequently on the agenda, too.

The most singular breakfast host may be the Norman Bird Sanctuary in Middletown. Here not all the eggs are on your plate. There are exhibits on local bird life, and you can follow your morning dining with a guided bird walk.

Generally, admission to May breakfasts ranges from $4 to $6 per adult and $2 to $3 per child. There are exceptions. Some take reservations, and others insist on them. At the most popular, such as the Oak Lawn Baptist Church, upwards of one thousand people may be served, and waiting is common.

By way of perspective, the first May breakfast at Oak Lawn Baptist Church in 1867 cost seventy-five cents per person. In 1998, the adult admission was $5.50, not much of an increase over the course of 131 years.

For More Information

You can receive a complete schedule of May breakfasts, with specific menus, prices, information about reservations, and name of the charity that is beneficiary of the income by contacting: Rhode Island Tourism Division, 1 West Exchange Street, Providence, RI 02903; (401) 222-2601.

May Breakfasts

9

The Maritime Center at Norwalk

A FOUR-YEAR-OLD GIRL STANDS WITH HER FACE PRESSED against an aquarium glass as a fish swims directly in front of her, mouth wide open and teeth exposed.

"The fishy smiled at me," the girl gleams.

With that fish's homely face, it was perhaps more of a snarl.

But if a four-year-old girl sees a smile, that's all that matters. There is nothing fishy about a kid enjoying herself.

The maritime center, devoted to the history and marine life of Connecticut's Long Island Sound, is made up of three parts: the aquarium; a maritime hall, which is a substantial museum devoted to life at sea; and an IMAX theater.

Anyone who visits should make the theater a priority. It's worth the extra charge. IMAX stands for "image maximum," and you may have seen IMAX theaters elsewhere. The most famous might be at the Smithsonian Institution's Air and Space Museum in Washington, D.C.

The screen here is six stories high and eight stories wide. When you watch a Coast Guard ship sail through a stormy sea on a rescue mission, you are virtually on the boat. When the camera scans the ocean floor, you are floating above the corals. When a surfer wipes out and hits bottom, you can nearly taste the salt and feel the sand.

To literally get a feel for ocean life, visit the touch tank in the aquarium, where a staffer is on duty to help out and offer information. See for yourself how rough a starfish is or how sharp the pointed tail of a horseshoe crab feels.

The horseshoe crab you see lying on his back isn't uncomfortable. He uses his tail to flip himself over and apparently likes it that way. Though you can see the clams and oysters, they can't see you— they have no eyes. Scallops, meanwhile, have lots of eyes, while sea stars (a.k.a. starfish) have eyes at the end of each arm. And yes, their arms do regenerate if one is lost.

Harbor seals live at the aquarium in a specially designed indoor/outdoor tank and are fed three times a day in public displays. Each has its own space to receive its food—herring and, to supply their need for water, a small fish called capelin. The seal-feeding staffers are happy to answer questions.

There is something to amuse kids in nearly every display, with or without smiling fishies. One exhibit, Waterworks, offers young ones the fun of playing in the bathtub without the bath. They can build a dam out of Legos or move toy boats in a stream to learn how water flow is affected by objects of differing shapes and sizes. In the maritime hall, youngsters and grown-ups, too, get a chance to test their sailing skills with a machine-made wind tunnel.

No oxymoron intended, but temporary exhibits are constants. In one exhibit on bogs which was there when we visited, children used a handheld cranberry scoop to try to catch up artificial berries buried among synthetic but realistic bog grass. It's hard work; no wonder cranberry workers now rely on automation.

There is more. Don't hesitate to chat with workers in the hall's boat shop as they practice the nearly extinct art of building wooden boats. You can watch swimming sharks and be glad they are safely behind glass. Then learn the

Spring

answer to this trivia question: What has no brain, no heart, no blood, and no lungs but has been around for 650 million years? No, not your boss. It's the wiggly jellyfish.

Also bear in mind that the center hosts an assortment of special programs for children as well as boat works courses and learning cruises in the warm-weather months.

FOR MORE INFORMATION

Location: The Maritime Center at Norwalk is at 10 North Water Street, on the banks of the Norwalk River. From Interstate 95, take exit 14 (northbound) or exit 15 (southbound).

Admission: A fee is charged.

Hours: Year-round, daily, except for Thanksgiving and Christmas.

Contact: The Maritime Center at Norwalk, 10 North Water Street, Norwalk, CT 06854; (203) 852-0700.

When in the area: The wild side of Fairfield County can be explored at the many nature centers (Chapter 11). In Wilton, to the north, is Weir Farm National Historic Site, comprising the home and studios of one of the nation's founding fathers of the American impressionist art movement (Chapter 21).

Lodging: Days Inn, 426 Main Avenue, Norwalk, CT; (203) 849-9828. Garden Park Motel, 351 Westport Avenue (Route 1), Norwalk, CT; (203) 847-7303. Ramada Hotel at River Park, 789 Connecticut Avenue, Norwalk, CT; (203) 853-3477. Silvermine Tavern (a 1785 country inn), 194 Perry Avenue, Norwalk, CT; (203) 847-4558.

The Maritime Center at Norwalk

10

Mr. Gillette's Valley

SOME OF MY EARLIEST MEMORIES ARE OF SUMMER DRIVES during the late 1950s through the lower Connecticut River Valley on Route 9, the road that paralleled the Connecticut River and took us from our home in hot, hazy West Hartford to our rental cottage by the shore in Old Saybrook. In the days before central air-conditioning became commonplace, many Hartfordites made similar pilgrimages down the meandering two-lane road on their way to clapboard beach cottages.

To me with my childhood attention span, the drive seemed agonizingly long, although my parents allowed for a midway stop at a hot dog stand called Pop's somewhere around Middletown. The view of East Haddam's swing bridge fascinated me and also broke up the monotony. So did the lonely, old Victorian-style Goodspeed Opera House that had fallen out of fashion. At the time, it was used as a grungy highway garage that was destined to have a wrestling match with the wrecking ball.

Once, we detoured to Hadlyme on the east side of the river and visited Gillette Castle, the monumental home of actor and playwright William Gillette, best known for his portrayal of detective Sherlock Holmes. I long recalled the castle's massive living room—our cottage would have fit comfortably inside it. And I couldn't forget all of Gillette's photos and ornaments of cats!

I recently journeyed back to the lower Connecticut River Valley, to this place of many of my childhood memories, a bit like Geraldine Page in *The Trip to Bountiful.*

But unlike Page's heartbreaking journey, I discovered a place that still thrives. The swing bridge is still there, and the country roads remain country roads, escaping the claws of the creeping urban sprawl. Or if you'd rather, you can make the most of your time by taking the new Route 9, the main highway that cuts travel time in half. The old Route 9 was renamed Route 9A before being changed again, to Route 154.

As a well-traveled adult, I saw Gillette's living room with different eyes from those I had as a youngster. It's a pleasing combination of majesty and warmth, fifty feet long, thirty feet wide, and nineteen feet high, with the atmosphere of a toasty lodge. The walls are of native stone, southern white oak, and raffia matting from the island of Java. It's the matting and the fireplace that warm the room, figuratively and literally.

One of the twenty-four rooms has been decorated to resemble the fictional Sherlock Holmes's headquarters at 221B Baker Street. It contains vials and a microscope on one table, piles of paperwork for the busy detective to pore over on another, and a lazy fiddle resting on an easy chair. Gillette had plenty of cats to go with that fiddle. He owned as many as twenty real ones at one time, and you can still see his many artificial ones made of porcelain and paper.

Following Gillette's lead, actors still come to this part of the state. The Goodspeed Opera House reopened as a working theater in 1963. It hardly resembles the unloved eyesore I recall from my travels during the Eisenhower era. The interior is a Victorian gem, with its period ladies' drinking parlor and hand-painted antique wallpaper. Musicals *Annie, Shenandoah,* and *Man of La Mancha* all premiered here.

And the clapboard homes I remember? They have not crumbled like those in Geraldine Page's Bountiful. The houses in the town of Essex that once sheltered sea captains support craft and specialty shops. And there's another throwback to the past, one that appeared long after I last came here. In 1971 the Valley Railroad opened and has been taking travelers on steam-train rides since. You relax in one of six coaches or, for an extra fee, inside the parlor car with its red swivel seats. There's also the option of extending your visit with an hour-long riverboat cruise.

There was one bit of Bountiful in my visit, though. Pop's Hot Dog Stand is gone, purposely destroyed in the late 1980s as part of a fire drill. But, one lost memory isn't bad over the course of thirty years of progress.

FOR MORE INFORMATION

Location: To reach Gillette Castle, take Route 82 west to River Road to the castle. From Route 9, exit 6 is the closest, but you have to take the car ferry across the river. Exit 7 is farther away, but you take a bridge.

Admission: A fee is charged for the castle; no charge to walk the expansive grounds.

Hours: Gillette Castle is open Memorial Day through Columbus Day, daily; Columbus Day through mid-December, weekends, including the Victorian holiday celebration (Chapter 49). Grounds are open year-round, daily.

Contact: Gillette Castle State Park, 67 River Road, East Haddam, CT 06423; (860) 526-2336.

Location: Goodspeed Opera House is on Route 82 at East Haddam Bridge.

Admission: A fee is charged for both performances and guided tours.

Hours: Guided tours are offered on a limited basis Monday and Saturday; call for specific tour times and theater schedule.

Mr. Gillette's Valley

Contact: Goodspeed Opera House, Goodspeed Landing, East Haddam, CT 06423; (860) 873-8664.

Location: Valley Railroad is one-quarter mile west of Route 9, exit 3, on Route 154. From Interstate 95, exit 69, take Route 9 north to exit 3 and head west on Route 154.
Admission: A fee is charged.
Hours: Mid-May through late October, with the most daily rides offered mid-June through Labor Day.
Contact: Valley Railroad Company, PO Box 452, Essex, CT 06426; (860) 767-0103.
Lodging: A cluster of quality B and Bs exists in the valley. Following is a sampling: Bishopsgate Inn (a Federal-style 1818 home), 7 Norwich Road, East Haddam, CT; (860) 873-1677. The Gelston House (an 1853 home), 8 Main Street, East Haddam, CT; (860) 873-1411. Griswold Inn (a colonial inn dating to 1776, one of the country's oldest), 36 Main Street, Essex, CT; (860) 767-1776. The Inn at Chester, 318 West Main Street, Chester, CT; (800) 949-7829 or (860) 526-9541.

Spring

11

Return to Nature

SPRING IN SOUTH CAROLINA ARRIVES ON SCHEDULE. WHEN the calendar says March 21, the azaleas are in bloom in Charleston and the lawns are green in Greenville.

Not so in New England, when the ground can still be covered with six inches of snow. The first dose of spring weather, when it finally does arrive, is like taking off a pair of too tight shoes.

It's only natural that when spring comes, New Englanders are dying to spend as much time outdoors as possible, to explore the woods, to examine the wildflowers, to walk the paths of nature.

It might seem ironic that perhaps southern New England's largest concentration of nature centers is in the region's most densely populated area—southwestern Connecticut. There are no fewer than seven such areas in Fairfield County or just over its border.

Following is a roundup of some of the major nature centers.

FOR MORE INFORMATION

The Nature Center for Environmental Activities: 10 Woodside Lane, PO Box 165, Westport, CT 06881. Hold a sea horse or let a crab crawl across your hand. Listen to the "ka-tunk" twang of a frog as you walk along the loop trail surrounding a typical Connecticut swamp. Admire the varied colors of wildflowers, such as the red trillium, the violet, and the spring beauty. Learn that fiddleheads are not Itzhak Perlman fanatics. Examine the habitats of Connecticut animals in three-dimensional, miniature model scenes. These are a few of the activities in which one can engage at this complex devoted to environmental education, preservation, and conservation. It was founded in 1958 and today consists of sixty-two acres with three miles of trails, a museum, a playground, and a picnic area. Open daily; afternoons only on Sunday. Admission is charged. (203) 227-7253.

Connecticut Audubon Society at Fairfield: 2325 Burr Street, Fairfield, CT 06430. As you might expect at an Audubon Center, there is an animal-care facility for injured birds with staff members who are happy to answer your questions. There is also the roughly 160-acre Roy & Margot Larsen Sanctuary with seven miles of walking trails and boardwalks. Markers explain the nature of the diverse topography that comprises the sanctuary—fields, marshes, streams, ponds, woods. Closed Mondays, open Sunday in fall and spring only. Admission is charged. (203) 259-6305. (For information on bird-watching here, see Chapter 35.)

Connecticut Audubon Birdcraft Museum: 314 Unquowa Road, Fairfield, CT 06430. Just a hummingbird's flight from downtown Fairfield is this museum with dioramas, a children's play corner, and dinosaur footprints. Established in 1924 as the first songbird sanctuary in the nation, this museum is a center for those wishing to learn about local birds and wildlife. After visiting, you can take an informative walk along the trails of the adjacent six-mile sanctuary. Open Wednesday through Sunday. Admission is charged. (203) 259-0416.

Flanders Nature Center: Church Hill and Flanders Road, PO Box 702, Woodbury, CT 06798-0702. The sprawling property comprises 1,300 acres, and there are about ten miles of nature trails where you might see wild turkeys,

Canada geese, foxes, and deer. In spring you might see resident ewes Rosie, Lola, and Gina get their annual haircuts. Consider taking a walk by the wildflowers in the woods or learning how maple syrup is made (see Chapter 4). The center is staffed Monday through Saturday, although trails are open seven days a week. Admission to the trails is free. Admission is charged for most programs. (203) 263-3711.

Bartlett Arboretum: 151 Brookdale Road, Stamford, CT 06903. Where can you see a thriving cactus collection 3,000 miles northeast of Arizona? At this arboretum operated by the University of Connecticut and a private foundation, you are invited to enter the 3,600-square-foot greenhouse and inspect the collection of cacti and succulents. You can also take a walk on the boardwalk through a swamp; stroll the grounds admiring collections of nut trees, conifers, and azaleas; or attend workshops on topics including sketching flowers and home gardening. Grounds open daily; visitor center open weekdays. Admission is free. (203) 322-6971.

Audubon Center in Greenwich: 613 Riversville Road, Greenwich, CT 06831. The birds join the bees in the center's interpretive building. A demonstration beehive and a bird observation window are two of the main attractions inside. Outside are eight miles of trails and 280 acres of woods, meadows, still ponds, and rushing streams. A mile away is the 127-acre Audubon Fairchild Garden, a wildlife sanctuary with an eight-mile trail network. Admission is charged. The Audubon Center is open daily except Monday. The Fairchild Garden is open daily. (203) 869-5272.

New Canaan Nature Center: 144 Oenoke Ridge, New Canaan, CT 06840. There are forty acres here with an herb garden, a solar greenhouse, an arboretum, and a wildflower garden. The herb garden alone is divided into several individual gardens; its culinary garden has separate salad and tea beds where common plants such as mints share space with edible blossoms of lemon marigolds and nasturtiums. For those with restless legs there are two miles of trails, including a 350-foot marsh boardwalk. For those with restless hands there is a Discovery Center gallery. (203) 966-9577.

When in the area: Have a look at the best works of both man and nature at Weir Farm National Historic Site (Chapter 21), or explore the natural life and legends of the sea at the Maritime Center at Norwalk (Chapter 9).

Lodging: Fairfield Motor Inn, 417 Post Road, Fairfield, CT; (800) 257-0496 or (203) 255-0491. Bridgeport Holiday Inn, 1070 Main Street, Bridgeport, CT; (203) 334-1234. Trumbull Marriott, 180 Hawley Lane, Trumbull, CT; (203) 378-1400. Homestead Inn (an elegant country inn dating to 1799), 420 Field Point Road, Greenwich, CT; (203) 869-7500. Stanton House Inn (a Stanford White–designed turn-of-the-century mansion-turned-inn), 76 Maple Avenue, Greenwich, CT; (203) 869-2110. Comfort Inn, 50 Ledge Road, Darien, CT; (203) 655-8211.

Spring

12

Mystic Seaport in Springtime

THE *CHARLES W. MORGAN*, AMERICA'S ONLY SURVIVING wooden whaling ship, commands the waterfront at Mystic Seaport in every season, in any weather. The floating national historic landmark, with its blubber pots and sardine-can double bunks, is the pride of this multi-building and -vessel museum located along the Mystic River by the Connecticut shoreline.

The boat, built in 1841, is also the setting for sail handling and other demonstrations which begin seasonally in April. Depending on the weather and number of crew on hand, from one to twelve sails might be set on the *Charles W. Morgan*. While most of the crew is aloft, one person stays on deck to explain the mechanics of sail setting to assembled visitors. You are invited to help out by pulling ropes on deck. Come in the less busy spring season, and your chances of being called on to lend a hand are even better.

Or listen for the words "Thar she blows," signaling the start of the whaling demonstration on board the *Morgan*. Visitors are asked to help haul a whaleboat on the *Morgan*'s davits if they wish, as the fifteen-minute-long demonstration nears an end. All the while, a sea chantey may be sung by the crew.

There are three other vessels docked in the Mystic River waiting to be toured. One is the *Joseph Conrad*, a Danish tall ship built in 1882 to train members of Denmark's merchant service.

Another is the *L. A. Dunton*, a 1921 Gloucester fishing schooner. The third is the *Sabino*, a 1908 coal-fired passenger ferry used for cruises up and down the Mystic River. And there are more than four hundred small craft preserved on land in buildings.

Mystic Seaport, of course, is more than boats. Anyone who attended grade school in Connecticut will remember field trips spent wandering into and out of the cooperage, the tavern, the one-room schoolhouse, the Buckingham House, and the other three-dozen-odd exhibit buildings that make up the prototypical 19th-century seaport town.

Come on a spring weekday and you might feel a sense of déjà vu. Mystic Seaport is still a magnet for school groups, and spring is their favorite time to visit. If you want your visit to be free from hordes of gum-cracking ten-year-olds in South Park T-shirts, plan to be here on a Saturday or Sunday.

In fact, the staff has designated April as Mystic Seaport Seniors Month. Discounts are offered to seniors on admission and in restaurants and the museum shop. Seniors are also permitted to bring up to four grandchildren, ages six to fifteen, with them for free. A family horse-and-carriage ride through the village is more leisurely in April than in summer, and visitors have a better opportunity to help out with village crafts such as butter making or spinning.

Said one interpreter, "You have a chance to get involved hands-on, something we can't offer guests when there are 5,000 people here."

Spring is also the season when special events begin in earnest. Memorial Day weekend is also Mystic Seaport's Lobsterfest. Visitors dine on platters of lobster (of course), cole slaw, corn on the cob, rolls, and either iced tea or lemonade as the museum's chantey men serenade them with songs of the sea.

On actual Memorial Day, known here by its 19th-century name, Decoration Day, a period memorial ceremony honoring soldiers who died in the Civil War is re-created. There is a short service, a reading of the Gettysburg Address, and a gathering of costumed Civil War veterans and dignitaries.

In addition, there is a re-creation of a symbolic event that took place in seaport towns and villages in the late 1800s. A wreath honoring army veterans is placed on a cannon by the Mystic River, and a second one is carried on a rowboat and left floating on the water in memory of navy men who died in the war. A trumpeter then plays "Taps" from the *Charles W. Morgan*'s deck, and three shots are fired from the wharf as the ceremony draws to a close.

On the cusp of the end of spring and the beginning of summer is the annual Sea Music Festival, in which both traditional and contemporary music is offered in concerts on the grounds. Bring the kids along for a special program of sea chanteys for children, or leave them at home and take the late-night pub crawl.

FOR MORE INFORMATION

Location: Mystic Seaport Museum is on Route 27, three-quarters of a mile south of Interstate 95, exit 90.
Admission: A fee is charged.
Hours: Year-round, daily, except Christmas Day.
Contact: Mystic Seaport Museum, 75 Greenmanville Avenue, PO Box 6000, Mystic, CT 06355-0990; (203) 572-0711.
When in the area: The Mystic Marinelife Aquarium is less than a mile away (Chapter 43).
Lodging: Best Western Sovereign Hotel—Mystic, 9 Whitehall Avenue, Mystic, CT; (860) 536-4281. Mystic Hilton, 20 Coogan Boulevard, Mystic, CT; (860) 572-0731. Comfort Inn of Mystic, 48 Whitehall Avenue, Mystic, CT; (860) 572-8531. Adams House (a 1790 home turned into a B and B), 382 Cow Hill Road, Mystic, CT; (860) 572-9551. Red Brook Inn (two colonial buildings turned into a B and B), 2750 Gold Star Highway, Mystic, CT; (860) 572-0349.

13

Hill-Stead Museum and the Stanley-Whitman House

IN 1901 AN INDUSTRIALIST NAMED ALFRED POPE BUILT A WHITE Colonial Revival mansion looking as luscious as a wedding cake in what was then rural Farmington, Connecticut. Inside he hung works by the most highly regarded artists of his era. Today it's known as Hill-Stead Museum.

Nearly two centuries earlier, John Stanley, son of one of the town's founders, built a wood-frame house in the colonial New England overhang style of architecture. It was still standing when Alfred Pope built his mansion, and it still stands today.

Spring might be the most inviting time to visit these homes. The gardens are blooming, and the country—albeit on the outskirts of suburbia—is still sweet and young.

Early in the spring, the trees and shrubs, such as the magnolias, flowering crab apple, and beauty bush, are busting out in blossoms at Hill-Stead. In May the daffodils are in bloom. In late spring the gardens are a comforter of pink and white, with roses and peonies showing their colors. Those who know gardens will be interested to hear that Hill-Stead's garden was designed by famed landscape architect Beatrix Farrand.

The landscape outside Hill-Stead would inspire any impressionist. It is on the inside that one can see the works of the actual artists. Hanging on the walls are the efforts of the greats: Monet, Manet, Degas, as well as Whistler and Cassatt.

Pope, born in 1842 in Maine, made his fortune as president of the Cleveland Malleable Iron Company. He became a serious art collector in the late 1880s, when impressionism was causing quite a stir over in Europe.

Stand in the drawing room and look at Monet's *Haystacks*. Step away from it and notice its three-dimensional effect. Pope bought Manet's *The Guitar Player* for $12,000 in 1894, at the time a record payment for the artist. In *Dancers in Pink* by Degas, girls wait anxiously backstage at a recital.

From the other side of the world are Japanese prints. They line a wall in the sitting room used by Alfred Pope's wife, Ada Brooks Pope. One print, *The Great Wave*, will look familiar. It has been reprinted many times, in various forms, and one child on our tour referred to it as the Ocean Spray picture, since it strongly resembles the cranberry juice company's logo.

The Popes spared no expense in obtaining decorative arts. On the mantel in the warm and dark second library is an ancient Corinthian vase, decorated with mythological beasts and dating to about 650 B.C. Try to locate all the secret drawers in the Chippendale secretary in the parlor bedroom. Our guide informed us, "The root word in secretary is 'secret.'" It makes sense.

The Stanley-Whitman House, a drive of perhaps five minutes away, tells a tale of colonial Farmington. Experts have put the construction date at around 1720. As at Hill-Stead, the garden here plays an important role.

We learned here that no matter what you did for a living in the 1700s, you were also a gardener. People ate and wore what they raised and grew in their gardens. Our docent—and the docents here are among the most knowledgeable we've come across anywhere—said that the residents would have spent as much time outdoors as possible.

But this was no tidy, suburban garden. There would have been animals roaming around on sloppy, muddy ground. On a hot day the stench could have knocked out a buzzard. Today, though, you will see a neatly arranged changing garden with colonial herbs such as thyme and sweet woodruff, and flowers such as blue irises and daylilies.

Indoors, dried herbs hang from beams in front of the kitchen fireplace. Note original kitchen utensils, including a Dutch oven, a spice box, a pipe box on the wall holding clay pipes smoked by the man (and woman) of the house (women routinely smoked tobacco), and a sugar snipper and sugar cone. We learned that the sugar cone came in royal blue paper, which was reused for dyeing materials.

The guided tour takes visitors both upstairs and downstairs. Spend time examining the displays in the visitor center, too. There is an authentic Early American lice comb used to free children's hair of the little blood-sucking insects, and a "wheel of time" which indicates what colonial activities were traditionally done in which month. In September, we learned, it was customary to bleed horses.

Various special events are scheduled at the Stanley-Whitman House, ranging from lectures on herbs and spices to an 18th-century corn roast.

For More Information

Location: Both sites can be reached by taking Interstate 84, exit 39, onto Route 4. To reach Hill-Stead Museum, take Route 4, then turn left onto Route 10 and then left again, onto Mountain Road. To reach Stanley-Whitman House, take Route 4, then turn left onto High Street.

Admission: A fee is charged for both sites.

Hours: Hill-Stead Museum is open year-round, daily, except Monday. The Stanley-Whitman House is open Wednesday through Sunday, afternoons only, May through October; and Sunday afternoon only in March, April, November, and December.

Contact: Hill-Stead Museum, 35 Mountain Road, Farmington, CT 06032; (860) 677-9064 or (860) 677-4787. The Stanley-Whitman House, 37 High Street, Farmington, CT 06032; (860) 677-9222.

When in the area: The long and often weird story of America's political history is placed under glass at the Museum of American Political Life in West Hartford (Chapter 31).

Lodging: Centennial Inn Suites, 5 Spring Lane, Farmington, CT; (800) 852-2052 or (860) 677-4647. Marriott Hotel–Farmington, 15 Farm Springs Road, Farmington, CT; (860) 678-1000. The Farmington Inn, 827 Farmington Avenue, Farmington, CT; (800) 648-9804 or (860) 677-2821. Barney House (a 19th-century manor turned B and B), 11 Mountain Spring Road, Farmington, CT; (860) 674-2796.

Summer

14

Reach the Beach

IF YOU INCLUDE THE BAY AND ALL THE INLETS, THE RHODE Island coastline alone is more than four hundred miles long. Stretched out, that would take you from Rhode Island to Virginia. Add the Connecticut coast and innumerable freshwater lakes and ponds, and we have tons of beaches for all tastes.

I asked people in state park and forest departments, along with tourism experts in Connecticut and Rhode Island, to name the five best beaches in each state. Then we asked for some undiscovered gems. Their answers follow.

Expect peak summer saltwater temperatures to range from the high sixties to the low seventies. Freshwater temperatures can be even warmer. At state beaches, plan on paying parking fees of $5 to $10, depending on the day. Charges at state park beaches are higher for nonresidents. At private beaches you might pay $5 to $15 to park. Also, bear in mind that many of the listed phone numbers are seasonal.

Rhode Island

The Top Five

1. **Misquamicut State Beach,** Westerly—This is a legendary stop for southern New Englanders, especially

those from Connecticut looking for high surf lacking along Long Island Sound. It's Rhode Island's largest state-owned beach, with more than a half mile of beach frontage. There are a huge parking lot, changing rooms, and bathrooms. At its eastern end, Misquamicut becomes Atlantic Beach, with the honky-tonk atmosphere kids love. (401) 596-9077.

2. **Scarborough State Beach,** Narragansett—Scarborough is popular with both families and teens. As Rhode Island's most used beach, it is wide and sandy with gazebos, picnic areas, changing rooms, bathrooms, and lots of parking. (401) 789-8013.

3. **Goosewing Beach,** Little Compton—If you are looking for sheer aesthetics, this is the place. It's a beauty and great for families. There is no parking lot; you park at Little Compton's town beach called South Shore Beach (rocky and not the prettiest) and walk the short distance here. (401) 635-4400.

4. **Narragansett Town Beach,** Narragansett—This popular sun-and-fun spot is wide, sandy, and home to some of the best surfing in the Northeast. At the beach are a picnic area and changing rooms. Within walking distance are a grocery store, restaurants, and public bathrooms. This is the only beach listed here charging both parking and admission fees. (401) 783-6430.

5. **Sachuest (Second) Beach,** Middletown—Just north of Newport, Sachuest gets a share of tourists, but it's less busy than Newport's Easton's (First) Beach. It is also less built up than Easton's and prettier, with 8,000 feet of wide, sandy frontage. You will find a concession area, picnic tables, bathrooms, changing rooms, and a sizable parking lot here. (401) 849-2822.

Summer

Three Hidden Gems

1. **East Beach,** Charlestown—Part of Ninigret Conservation Area, this barrier beach is three miles long and an unspoiled beauty. It is also great for bird-watching (see Chapter 35), but lacking in facilities; the parking lot holds fewer than 100 cars, so come early in the day. (401) 364-7000.

2. **Quonochontaug Beach,** Westerly—This pretty beach is part of Quonochontaug Conservation Area and one of the state's last that is undeveloped and privately owned. Extras are lacking here, too; go for isolation and the setting. (401) 783-0687.

3. **Pulaski State Park Beach,** Chepachet—Recommending a freshwater beach in a saltwater-fringed state might seem a bit like suggesting Foxwoods Casino to Nevada residents. The advantages of an inland lake such as this are warmer and calmer waters than that of the ocean. And you won't find pretty wooded hills along the seacoast. (401) 568-2013.

Connecticut

The Top Five

1. **Hammonasset Beach State Park,** Madison—There are three big ocean state beaches in Connecticut, and this is the biggest. It is two miles long and has facilities for everything from picnicking and hiking to scuba diving and fishing. There is a large campground, and adjacent is a large salt-marsh natural area with native flora and fauna. (203) 245-2785.

2. **Rocky Neck State Park,** Niantic—The second is this crescent-shaped beach, a half mile long and with picnic tables, hiking trails, a boardwalk, observation platforms, and a campground. On the grounds is a lodge built by the WPA in the 1930s. Come early on weekends and really hot days. (860) 739-5471.

3. **Sherwood Island State Park,** Westport—The last of the big three is the only state park beach in Fairfield County, which means that Sherwood Island draws a substantial share of sunbathers from New York state. The water isn't as clear as you will find closer to Rhode Island, but making up for that is a beautiful oak grove for picnicking. (203) 226-6983.

4. **Sandy Beach,** Morris—Connected to the White Memorial Foundation near Litchfield, the secluded cove is part of Bantam Lake, largest freshwater lake in the state. The beach measures about eight hundred feet long, and the water can reach up to eighty degrees in the heat of summer. Extras include a picnic area, volleyball courts, and bathhouses. (860) 567-0857.

5. **Bigelow Hollow State Park,** Union—Perhaps the prettiest inland beach in Connecticut, this one on the shore of Mashapaug Lake near Interstate 84 is surrounded by woods and hills and few man-made eyesores. The water is beautiful, and the beach is sandy and gravelly. On hot weekends this one tends to fill up, and it also draws a younger crowd than many other lake beaches. (860) 928-9200.

Three Hidden Gems

1. **Bluff Point State Park,** Groton—This is not the place to go if you want picnic areas and concession stands. It is

the place to go to relax along the ocean in an all-natural setting. One parks at the entrance and walks a mile and a half to reach the beach. The water is among the clearest of any Connecticut state beaches. (860) 445-1729.

2. **Mount Tom State Park,** New Preston—On warm summer days, the temperature of the water here can easily range between seventy-five and eighty degrees. It is also super clear, and beach visitation usually tops out at a few hundred people. In addition, you can climb to the summit of the stone lookout tower on the top of Mount Tom, 1,291 feet high. Other activities include scuba diving, picnicking, and boating. (860) 868-2592.

3. **Uncas Pond,** Lyme—Why travel this far south and not head to the brine at Rocky Neck State Park? Consider that this is a clear, clean body of water surrounded by Nehantic State Forest. It's not for those seeking a sprawling beach filled with humanity; the beach is small but undeveloped, and there are hardly any man-made distractions. That also means no facilities, and you have to park on State Forest Road—half paved, half gravel—and walk to the beach. Because of the park's remote location, there is no phone; it is overseen by the staff at Rocky Neck State Park. (860) 739-5471.

Reach the Beach

15

Maritime Newport

NOTHING SEEMS TO SAY SUMMER LIKE THE OCEAN, AND
Newport has long had a close relationship with salt water.
The Vanderbilts sailed on it, the navy sailed on it, and you
can sail on it.

The most celebrated sailors who manned ships here did
so for half a century as part of the America's Cup competition. They and others of their kind are honored in the
Museum of Yachting where intricate color sketches of America's Cup contenders, from *America* in 1851 to *America 3* in
1992, decorate the walls.

Visitors also learn a surprising fact: the America's Cup
competition, so often associated with this city on Narragansett Bay, was held here for only a little more than fifty
years. While the United States controlled the cup from the
race's inception in 1851 until its loss to Australia in 1982,
the races were held in lower New York Bay until 1930.

There are boatloads of relics of America's Cup contenders,
too. Consider ships' wheels, compasses, 1930s deck shoes,
and a 1930s plainmeter. What's a plainmeter? It's a device
used to mechanically measure irregular shapes. True, we
were never asked that on our SATs, but you never know
when you will wind up on *Jeopardy*.

The grittier side of yachting is preserved in the museum's
hall of fame for single-handed sailors. It is here that you read
stories of courage and, to some minds, lunacy. Joshua

Slocum voyaged around the world from 1895 to 1898, the first in the world to do it solo. Ann Davison became the first woman to sail alone across the Atlantic in the 1950s after her husband died in a boating accident. On view is her left-handed octant and a photograph of a triumphant Davison in her twenty-three-foot sloop, the *Felicity Ann*.

There are numerous boats on display, inside and outside the museum, and there is a boat restoration area where wooden yachts are repaired and maintained.

The ways of boating have been taught here for many years. The Naval War College, oldest in the world, was established in Newport in 1884 and is the highest educational institution in the U.S. Navy. Its Naval War College Museum, located in what was built in 1820 as Newport's poorhouse, recognizes the Naval Center and local navy history.

The "Fish" on view in the museum has no fins or gills. It is the first self-propelled torpedo made in the United States and dates to 1869. It has a local connection: in the years immediately following the Civil War, the Naval Torpedo Station, the first naval laboratory, was established on nearby Goat Island. Keeping the "Fish" company is a cross section of the Mark-14 torpedo, the country's premier submarine torpedo used during World War II. A legend next to the Mark-14 identifies such parts as rudder bearings, head joint, gyro reducer, and flange. I have no idea what those mean either.

Intricate ship models, vintage photos, and navy recruitment posters tell tales of earlier times. So do the Indian clubs, appearing like bowling pins that went through the wringer. They were used by naval trainees in the 1890s. Be sure to take a look at the medicine bottles, hauled up from the deep and covered with barnacles.

To take to the waves, consider the following:

Summer

Madeleine, a seventy-foot schooner, sails four times daily on two-hour cruises from Bannister's Wharf; (800) 395-1343 or (401) 849-3033.

Adirondack, a seventy-eight-foot schooner, also sails four times daily on two-hour cruises; (401) 846-1600, extension 221.

Sailing cruises of one to two hours can be taken through: Sight Sailing of Newport, (401) 849-3333; Newport Sailing School and Cruises Ltd., (401) 683-2738; the motor sailer *Woiee*, (401) 862-1397; and the catamaran *Flyer*, (800) TO-FLYER (863-5937) or (401) 848-2100.

For hour-long harbor cruises, try the M/V *Spirit of Newport*, (401) 849-3575; the M/V *Amazing Grace*, (401) 847-9109; and Viking Tours, (401) 847-6921.

FOR MORE INFORMATION

Location: The Museum of Yachting is located behind the fort in Fort Adams State Park. To reach it from the center of Newport, take Thames Street south; turn right onto Wellington Avenue and follow onto Halidon Avenue, then Harrison Avenue to the park entrance.

Admission: A fee is charged to enter the park, as well as to enter the museum.

Hours: Daily, mid-May through October; by appointment in winter.

Contact: Museum of Yachting, PO Box 129, Newport, RI 02840; (401) 847-1018.

Location: The Naval War College Museum is located inside Gate 1 of the Naval Education and Training Center. Follow

Route 114 north from the center of Newport to the entrance to the Naval Center.

Admission: No charge.

Hours: Weekdays, year-round, and weekdays and weekend afternoons in summer.

Contact: Naval War College Museum, 686 Cushing Road, Newport, RI 02841-1207; (401) 841-4052 or (401) 841-1317.

When in the area: Newport's famous mansions (Chapter 3), the International Tennis Hall of Fame (Chapter 19), and Touro Synagogue National Historic Site and some of the oldest houses in town (Chapter 37) are also open to the public.

Lodging: This is the B and B capital of southern New England. A partial list of Newport B and Bs includes: Cliffside Inn (former home of artist Beatrice Turner and repository for many of her works), 2 Seaview Avenue; (800) 845-1811 or (401) 847-1811. The Wayside, 406 Bellevue Avenue; (401) 847-0302. The Jailhouse Inn (a restored colonial jail), 13 Marlborough Street; (401) 847-4638. Brinley Victorian Inn, 23 Brinley Street; (800) 999-8523 or (401) 849-7645. The Willows, 8-10 Willow Street; (401) 846-5486.

There is also a B and B service listing rooms in more than 150 private homes, inns, and guest houses: Anna's Victorian Connection, 5 Fowler Avenue, Newport, RI 02840; (800) 884-4288 or (401) 849-2489.

Conventional motels in Newport include: Motel 6, 249 J. T. Connell Highway; (401) 848-0600. Best Western Mainstay Inn, 151 Admiral Kalbfus Road; (401) 849-9880. Newport Harbor Hotel & Marina, 49 America's Cup Avenue; (401) 847-9000.

16

Leaders of Lebanon

IF YOU THINK THE CREEPING MEGALOPOLIS HAS REACHED every piece of real estate from Washington to Boston, come to Lebanon, Connecticut. This small town in the eastern part of the state had a major role in the Revolutionary War, and it doesn't look much different from the way it did then.

As in many other New England towns, a green dominates the town center. But this one is a colossus. It extends a mile in length and resembles the sprawling pastureland it was in colonial days. During the war it was also a training ground; French troops camped on it during the winter of 1780–81.

Bordering the green are homes that were here when the troops were camped out and eating fire cake and water. There is the home of Jonathan Trumbull, respectfully called "Brother Jonathan" by George Washington and the only colonial governor who became a state governor. Trumbull was also the only colonial governor to support the war for independence. He lived and worked in a two-story, white frame house facing the green. Such illustrious Revolutionary-era figures as Washington, Adams, Rochambeau, Franklin, and Lafayette visited this house, and George Washington really did sleep here. Take a look at the original floorboards in the guest room where Washington slept; they are long and wide and about 255 years old.

In the dining room is a secret doorway hiding a narrow staircase. You can't climb it, but you see where it leads—to the governor's office, where Trumbull conducted official colonial business during wartime. The lone window is placed high on the wall, so bullets from a rebellious Tory or British soldier would pass far above Trumbull's head.

Much of the official business of war was conducted a bit farther west on the common at the small red building today known as the Revolutionary War Office. Before it served its martial purpose, it was Jonathan Trumbull's store. Inscribed on a plaque above the big fireplace in one of the two rooms are the following words: "During the War of the Revolution Governor Jonathan Trumbull and the Council of Safety held more than eleven hundred meetings in this Building and here also came many distinguished officers of the Continental Army and French Allies."

Inside are relics of war long ago such as old maps, a sword, and a powder horn. There are also relics of domesticity, such as a hetchel (used to break flax) and a cobbler's bench. Another display is devoted to artifacts found during nearby excavations: pottery shards, nails, a pair of pliers, and the like.

Behind Governor Trumbull's house on the south side of the green is the birthplace of another notable revolutionary, but not one of war fame. William Beaumont, born in 1785, was a medical revolutionary, sort of the George Washington of gastrointestinal physiology. While an army doctor, he attended a French Canadian fur trapper who was shot in the stomach. The wound never completely healed, the patient's stomach remained exposed, and Beaumont made use of this unusual situation to conduct medical studies. He published a landmark book on the physiology of digestion in 1833 and became known as the premier pioneer in the field.

Beaumont settled in Saint Louis and practiced medicine until his death in 1853 at the age of sixty-seven. The French Canadian trapper with the vulnerably exposed stomach outlived him by fifteen years.

For fear of vandalism, Beaumont's birthplace was moved to this location from a more remote part of Lebanon. Enter to see items not found in your typical colonial home. The tools of the medical trade in the early 19th century are in a glass cabinet. There is a monaural stethoscope, made of ebonized wood and looking more like a bud vase. There is also a colorful anatomy chart, circa 1812, and a dentist's tooth-puller, with a black handle and a hook-shaped bottom used to yank out one's tooth. Ouch!

The latest vintage home to open here is the refurbished and repainted home of Jonathan Trumbull Jr., also facing the green. Like his father, he was also a governor. Period furnishings and changing exhibits fill the halls.

(Actually, the most famous Trumbull is not represented by any house here. He is John, another son of the governor and the country's most famous Revolutionary-era artist whose best known work is *The Declaration of Independence*.)

FOR MORE INFORMATION

Location: Lebanon is at the junction of Routes 87 and 207. From Interstate 395, take Route 2 east to exit 25. Take Route 32 north for an eye blink to Route 87 toward Lebanon.

Admission A fee is charged to view the Governor Jonathan Trumbull House. Donation requested to view the Revolutionary War Office and Dr. William Beaumont House.

Hours: Governor Jonathan Trumbull House is open Tuesday through Saturday, afternoons only, mid-May through mid-October. The Revolutionary War Office is open weekend afternoons, Memorial Day through August, and Sunday afternoon in September. Dr. William Beaumont House is open Saturday afternoon, mid-May through mid-October. Call or check locally for hours to the Jonathan Trumbull Jr. house.

Contact: The Lebanon Historical Society, PO Box 151, Lebanon, CT 06249; (860) 642-7247.

When in the area: The dice are always rolling at Foxwoods Resort and Casino. Take Route 87 south to Route 2 south and follow the sounds of money changing hands (Chapter 51).

Lodging: Ramada Hotel, 10 Laura Boulevard, Norwich, CT; (860) 889-5201. Rosemont Suites, 181 West Town Street, Norwich, CT; (860) 889-2671. Norwich Inn & Spa, 607 West Thames Street (Route 32), Norwich, CT; (800) 275-4772 or (860) 886-2401. Hayward House Inn (B and B), 35 Hayward Avenue, Colchester, CT; (860) 537-5772.

17

Block Island

WE STRETCHED OUT ON A BEACH UNDER THE SHELTERING mass of the 163-foot-high chalky cliffs known as Mohegan Bluffs, where we watched the waves lap the shore in a reassuring monotony.

There were no concession stands.

There were no boom boxes.

Just us, our peace of mind, the sky, the sun, the sand, the waves.

The bluffs were a barrier, shielding us from the world's distractions. We had no radio—who wanted to hear the news?

This is Block Island.

If you desire hordes of humanity and funky shops, go to Provincetown. If you want beautiful people, where the men look like Richard Gere and the women like Julia Roberts, take the ferry to the Vineyard. There might be people who are beautiful on Block Island, but not the beautiful people.

The island is certainly not undiscovered. It *is* busy in summer, some areas more so than others. The chamber of commerce estimates that about 15,000 visitors a day in July and August inhabit the island. Most crowded is Old Harbor, the commercial center where the ferries from the mainland dock. But you will run into joggers, inline skaters, bicyclers, and motorists throughout the island.

The chamber recommends that weekenders save the $40 or so that it costs to transport a car back and forth on the ferry by leaving their cars behind. The island beckons bicyclers, and there are plenty of places to rent a bike. Those who prefer foot power are just as welcome. If you really need car transportation, taxicabs are available, and the price of a couple of cab rides is just a fraction of the cost of taking your car on the ferry.

The Victorian-era hotels and inns are vestiges of Block Island's lengthy history as a premier resort. People have been vacationing here for more than a century and a half. A Block Island historian wrote, "The first hotel for boarders from abroad was opened in 1842 by Mr. Alfred Card, one hundred and eighty years from the first settlement by sixteen families. There Mr. Card 'set the first excursion table for boarders of pleasure' ever furnished on the Island."

Block Island's past can be further inspected at two lighthouses and a historical museum. The Southeast Light, atop Mohegan Bluffs, dates from 1875 and was moved about 240 feet back from the bluffs in the mid-1990s to prevent it from becoming a victim of eroded shorefront. It resembles a humble brick cottage with an attached lighthouse, like a garage on a suburban split-level house. The other, North Light, is home to a maritime environmental center and museum.

The museum at the Block Island Historical Society shows off vintage quilts, photographs, and kitchen implements (including a huge cookie cutter). Wonder what you would have worn had you vacationed here 100 years ago? A slew of turn-of-the-century clothing is on view.

But those who come in summer want beaches, and there are twenty miles of public ones. The most visited are in the three-mile-long stretch known as Crescent Beach, a group name for many numerous small ones. Included is the popular family-oriented Fred Benson Town Beach. Here you will find rest rooms, showers, a snack bar, and a place to rent umbrellas to ward off the sweltering summer sun. It is about a ten-minute walk from the ferry dock.

For maximum exposure try the beach at Black Rock, at the island's southwest point. Though technically illegal, nude bathing is common here. Most of the island's ocean beaches are unnamed and can be found serendipitously. The water temperature is mild by New England standards, reaching a peak of seventy to seventy-five degrees. For even warmer water, try the inland beaches at Sachem Pond and Sands Pond, where the temperatures can be five degrees higher.

FOR MORE INFORMATION

Location: The main Block Island ferry leaves from Point Judith, Rhode Island, year-round. It has a capacity of 1,500 persons and thirty passenger cars. Reservations are needed for cars but not for pedestrians. For the busy summer season, make auto reservations at least one month in advance. Even at peak times, there is usually no more than a thirty-minute wait to board. But to assure yourself of not missing the boat, be at Point Judith an hour ahead of departure time. Sailing time is approximately an hour and ten minutes. There is also a summer auto ferry to Block Island from New London, Connecticut, leaving the mainland once each day. Sailing time for the New London ferry is about two hours.

Contact: Block Island Chamber of Commerce, Drawer D, Block Island, RI 02807; (800) 383-2474 or (401) 466-2982. Ferry information: Interstate Navigation Company, Box 482, New London, CT 06320; (860) 442-7891 in Connecticut, (401) 783-4613 in Rhode Island.

Lodging: All the following are on Block Island: Beach House B and B, Crescent Beach; (800) 419-3228 or (401) 466-2924. The Dewey Cottage, Ocean Avenue; (800) 330-3155 or (401) 466-3155. Gables Inn, Dodge Street; (401) 466-2213 or (401) 466-7721. The High View Inn, Connecticut Avenue; (401) 466-5912. Manisses Hotel and 1661 Inn, Spring Street; (401) 466-2063 or (401) 466-2421. The Spring House Hotel, Spring Street; (401) 466-5844 or (401) 466-2633.

Block Island

18

Music Alfresco

A LOAF OF BREAD, A JUG OF WINE, AND MAYBE A BUCKET OF the Colonel's best are the needed ingredients to complement a day or evening of music in the open air. Most outdoor concert venues welcome picnickers, and you are encouraged to bring blankets, beach chairs, or anything else you wish to park your backside on while listening to the best of classics, pops, and show tunes. To round out the trip, spend your time checking out the attraction hosting the event or exploring other nearby sights.

In Hartford, Trinity College is the setting for weekly Wednesday-evening concerts performed on the college's carillon. Folks gather on the quad to hear approximately ninety-minute-long stretches of show tunes, hymns, classical melodies, or original pieces. Preceding the outdoor concerts for much of the summer are chamber concerts of about forty-five minutes taking place inside the Trinity College chapel.

Contact: Trinity College Chapel, 300 Summit Street, Hartford, CT 06106-3100; (860) 297-2001.

Also in Hartford is the Evelyn Preston Memorial Fund Concert Series, where devotees of just about any music will likely find something that grabs them over the course of the summer. Concerts have featured jazz, salsa, bluegrass, classical, chamber, and rock and are held in venues throughout the city. Goodwin Park,

Elizabeth Park, Keney Park, Trinity College, and Charter Oak landing on the riverfront have all been settings.

Contact: Yvonne Harris, 25 Stonington Street, Hartford, CT 06106; (860) 722-6488.

To the south, New Haven has its own outdoor concert series, called Picnic Performances. The concerts are informal and draw a few hundred people each at different settings throughout the city. Says a representative of the series, "Our mission is to encourage park use. A lot of people are afraid of their parks, but they shouldn't be. We usually try to match musical style with specific neighborhood parks." Those styles have included gospel, reggae, classical, and folk rock.

Contact: Picnic Performances, 850 Grand Avenue, New Haven, CT 06511; (203) 773-1777.

The summer music series at Harkness Memorial State Park in coastal Waterford is appropriately tagged Sounds on the Sound. Classical and jazz musicians play against a background of the smooth waters of Long Island Sound. You can sit in a tent or on the grass, and the most elegant picnics are awarded prizes. An evening buffet is also served; reservations required. There have been some big names here such as Chick Corea, Emanuel Ax, The Temptations, and the Manhattan Transfer.

Contact: Summer Music, Inc., 300 Captain's Walk, Suite 503, New London, CT 06320; (860) 442-9199.

Come early for a seat on the lawn at the Bartlett Arboretum in Stamford for free outdoor concerts featuring a wide range of musical styles including jazz, classical, and barbershop. Extra time? Take a walk along the trails, or admire the gardens.

Contact: Bartlett Arboretum, 151 Brookdale Road, Stamford, CT 06903-4199; (203) 322-6971.

In Danbury is the Charles Ives Center for the Arts, on the Westside Campus of Western Connecticut State University. This cultural center brings true music legends of all styles to the great outdoors of the western end of the Constitution

Summer

State. Names such as Ray Charles, Gerry Mulligan, Tammy Wynette, Donna Summer, the Manhattan Transfer, and Skitch Henderson and the New York Pops from Carnegie Hall have graced the eight-sided pavilion that seems to float placidly in a pond. Those with sharp memories may recall Henderson as the conductor of Johnny Carson's *Tonight Show* Band in the 1960s.

As at the more famous Tanglewood in the Massachusetts Berkshires, Ives Center guests have a choice of sitting under cover or on the lawn. Lawn seating is more fun. You can stretch out, and you are truly under the stars. But if it rains, you get wet. Decisions. Decisions.

Contact: The Charles Ives Center, PO Box 2957, Danbury, CT 06813; (203) 797-4002.

The plush mansion and plentiful arboretum at Blithewold Mansion & Gardens in Bristol, Rhode Island, hosts Summer Concerts by the Bay. Six concerts take place over the summer, two each in June, July, and August, one indoors and one outdoors in each month. Classical music highlights the indoor concerts which can seat about 125, including the overflow section. The outdoor concerts take place on the great lawn and average crowds of about 400 but can hold more. Swing bands such as local favorites Avenue A, the area folk-and-Celtic group called Pendragon, brass bands, or vocal pops performers entertain outdoors in a less formal atmosphere. Take along a picnic for the outdoor shows.

Contact: Blithewold Mansion & Gardens, 101 Ferry Road, Bristol, RI 02809-0716; (401) 253-2707.

Music Al fresco

19

Tennis, Everyone?

I AM STANDING AGAINST THE NET, SANDWICHED BETWEEN tennis-playing brothers Luke and Murphy Jensen, watching a ball fly off their racquets as they volley. I follow the trajectory of the ball, looking upwards or sideways, and I am ready to duck as one ball is aimed squarely at my teeth.

No need, though. I am in the International Tennis Hall of Fame in Newport, Rhode Island. The Jensen brothers are on film on two screens facing each other and I am on a simulated tennis court, complete with official's chair on the side, in the middle of a high-tech exhibit in this major sport museum, much of it redesigned and renovated in the summers of 1995 and 1996.

With tennis's hall of fame located here, one doesn't need to raise a racquet to enjoy the game. Newport is tennis's Cooperstown, and anyone can soak up the action. Those who do want to play, however, will find public tennis courts throughout the state. There are, in fact, public courts at the hall of fame. The thirteen grass courts are the only competition grass courts in the nation open to the public.

And while the museum interior now celebrates the high-tech look in all its glory, its exterior is a throwback to the days when Queen Victoria ruled in Britain and tennis was the gentlemen's game for Harvard-educated members of high society. Turrets and towers overlook a horseshoe piazza in this building designed in 1880 as the Newport

Casino by famed Gilded Age architects McKim, Mead and White.

The Newport Casino was built as a social and recreational club for New York newspaper publisher James Gordon Bennett. In this case, the name "casino" has nothing to do with gambling. It comes from the Italian word *casina*, meaning "farmstead" or "little house," and in its prime this Casino hosted archery, billiards, bowling, dining, dancing, horse shows, and concerts in addition to both lawn and court tennis. Its claim to court fame, however, is the first U.S. National Lawn Tennis Championships which occurred here in 1881. The tourney continues today in Flushing, New York, as the U.S. Open.

What better place to house the shrine to tennis greats? The members' names and biographical sketches are memorialized on rectangular plaques near the museum entrance, and it is here one can learn about everyone from Chris Evert to Richard Sears, winner of that first tournament in 1881.

It is at the push of a button that one can learn about the nuances of the game, its history, and its controversies. Push a button and watch on a monitor as Ken Rosewall faces Rod Laver in the finals of a 1972 matchup. Push a button and learn why high-tech racquets may help the women's game but hinder the men's game. Push a button and learn how courtship had a large role in promoting the popularity of the court game 100 years ago.

Then sit in front of a television monitor where the following quote from tennis pioneer James Dwight appears: "Win quietly, lose quietly and don't get angry," followed by clips of jubilant winners and tantrums thrown by the likes of Nastase, Connors, and McEnroe. Can everyone enjoy tennis? Keep watching as clips are shown of wheelchair tennis, seniors playing tennis, and a kitten bandying about a tennis ball and nudging it with his little pink nose.

The other way to enjoy the court game is by actively participating yourself. A partial listing of public tennis courts in Rhode Island follows:

Summer

Providence: Roger Williams Park, ten courts

East Providence: Pierce Field, four courts

Pawtucket: Slater Park, 10 courts

Cranston: Park View Junior High, four courts

Warwick: Mickey Stevens Sports Complex, eight courts

Bristol: Mount Hope High School, six courts

Coventry: Paine Field, four courts

Cumberland: Courier Field, two courts

West Greenwich: Exeter/West Greenwich Junior/Senior High, six courts

Newport: Aquidneck Park, four courts; and International Tennis Hall of Fame, thirteen courts

For More Information

Location: The International Tennis Hall of Fame is located at 194 Bellevue Avenue, just south of its junction with Memorial Boulevard.

Admission: A fee is charged.

Hours: Year-round, daily, except for Thanksgiving, Christmas, and New Year's Day. The hall's grass courts are open to the public mid-May through early October.

Contact: International Tennis Hall of Fame, 194 Bellevue Avenue, Newport, RI 02840; (401) 849-3990. For court availability, call (401) 846-0642.

When in the area: Most of Newport's renowned mansions are on Bellevue Avenue (Chapter 3). The Touro Synagogue and colonial homes built when Newport was one of America's mightiest seaports can be toured (Chapter 37), as can museums devoted to the city's maritime history (Chapter 15).

Lodging: This is the B and B capital of southern New England. A partial list of Newport B and Bs includes: Cliff-side Inn (former home of artist Beatrice Turner and repository for many of her works), 2 Seaview Avenue; (800) 845-1811 or (401) 847-1811. The Wayside, 406 Bellevue Avenue; (401) 847-0302. The Jailhouse Inn (a restored colonial jail), 13 Marlborough Street; (401) 847-4638. Brinley Victorian Inn, 23 Brinley Street; (800) 999-8523 or (401) 849-7645. The Willows, 8-10 Willow Street; (401) 846-5486.

There is also a B and B service listing rooms in more than 150 private homes, inns, and guest houses: Anna's Victorian Connection, 5 Fowler Avenue, Newport, RI 02840; (800) 884-4288 or (401) 849-2489.

Conventional motels in Newport include: Motel 6, 249 J. T. Connell Highway; (401) 848-0600. Best Western Mainstay Inn, 151 Admiral Kalbfus Road; (401) 849-9880. Newport Harbor Hotel & Marina, 49 America's Cup Avenue; (401) 847-9000.

Summer

20

Getting Jollies on the Trolleys

OLD-TIME TROLLEYS ARE RARITIES NOWADAYS, EXCEPT IN Connecticut. In the state are two museums devoted exclusively to the bangling, jangling, old-time transit, located at the head and foot of Interstate 91 in the state.

Connecticut Trolley Museum

A yellow open trolley car, once part of a fleet that carried passengers to New Haven's Yale Bowl, rumbles through the woods in the Warehouse Point section of East Windsor near the Massachusetts border. Inside you might take in the craftsmanship of mahogany woodwork and the nostalgia of car cards with advertisements for products such as Wrigley's gum or mustache wax, while listening to a commentary and perhaps a bit of corny humor from the conductor. ("There was once a fight on this trolley. The conductor punched a ticket.")

The car cruises along tracks through the woods of northern Connecticut for a twenty-minute-long round trip of three miles. Your ticket is good for unlimited rides, and your visit includes a look inside the restoration shop and the visitor center museum, a final resting place for items saved from the trolley graveyard, including old transfers, a brass plate from a generator, and a big three-wheel velocipede, sort of a bicycle on steroids from the 1860s created just to run on tracks. Depending on staffing, you may be able to take a guided tour of the restoration shop and visitor center.

Other operating trolleys include a Montreal observation car used in warm weather only, and a 1922-era New Orleans car used in the movie *A Streetcar Named Desire*. If your name is Stella, this is your car.

Shore Line Trolley Museum

At the other end of Interstate 91 is the Shore Line Trolley Museum, which according to museum director George Boucher was the first such museum to operate on tracks already in place. (Other museums had the collections first and laid tracks later.) Created in 1947, the museum now boasts about one hundred pieces of equipment.

Rides are given on any of seven cars. In warm weather you might cruise along in a 1911 open car once ridden by local residents, or a convertible car that ran through the streets of Brooklyn, New York, as far back as 1906. (Trivia buffs, pay attention. In the early part of the century there were so many trolleys in Brooklyn that the local baseball team was called the Trolley Dodgers. The name was later shortened to the Dodgers.)

In cooler weather, there are a couple of closed cars from the 1920s for your riding pleasure. As at the Connecticut Trolley Museum, rides are about three miles long and last twenty minutes. You don't get to see Long Island Sound, since the ride stops about three blocks from the water, but you do ride past a substantial portion of salt marsh along the East Haven River.

The tour here is guided and takes you through two car barns and the restoration shop. There is one volunteer conductor on staff, a man in his seventies, who once operated trolleys for a living. Sadly, folks like these are becoming few and far between. Museum director George Boucher grew up around trolleys. He recalls family visits to his grandfather, a trolley supervisor in the 1940s. Boucher has been interested in "anything on rails" ever since.

FOR MORE INFORMATION

Location: For the Connecticut Trolley Museum, from Interstate 91, exit 45, head a half mile east on Route 140 (North Road) to the museum.

Admission: A fee is charged.

Hours: Weekends only January through Memorial Day and Labor Day to Thanksgiving; daily Memorial Day through Labor Day, and the day after Thanksgiving through January 1.

Contact: Connecticut Trolley Museum, 58 North Road, PO Box 360, East Windsor, CT 06088; (860) 627-6540.

When in the area: The New England Air Museum preserves classic aircraft near Bradley International Airport (Chapter 45).

Lodging: Holiday Inn Express, 260 Main Street, East Windsor, CT; (860) 627-6585. Ramada Inn, 161 Bridge Street, East Windsor, CT; (860) 623-9411. Red Roof Inn, 5 Hazard Avenue, Enfield, CT; (860) 741-2571. Motel 6, 11 Hazard Avenue, Enfield, CT; (860) 741-3685.

Location: Shore Line Trolley Museum is located near the green in East Haven. From Interstate 91 northbound, take exit 51; southbound, take exit 52, then follow signs to the museum.

Admission: A fee is charged.

Hours: Sunday in April; Saturday and Sunday in May; daily Memorial Day through Labor Day; weekends September,

Getting Jollies on the Trolleys

October, and late November through late December; and Sunday the rest of November.

Contact: Shore Line Trolley Museum, 17 River Street, East Haven, CT 06512; (203) 467-6927.

When in the area: In New Haven is Yale University and its abundance of museums (Chapter 46). In Branford and Guilford are two of Connecticut's premier craft centers (Chapter 5).

Lodging: Holiday Inn Express, 30 Frontage Road, East Haven, CT; (203) 469-5321. Residence Inn by Marriott, 3 Long Wharf Drive, New Haven, CT; (203) 777-5337. Motel 6, 320 East Main Street (Route 1), Branford; (203) 483-5828. MacDonald's Motel, 565 East Main Street (Route 1), Branford; (203) 488-4381.

Summer

21

Weir Farm National Historic Site

THE AMERICAN IMPRESSIONIST MOVEMENT BEGAN RIGHT HERE in Connecticut, and one of the principals was Julian Weir, known among art lovers as J. Alden Weir. His farm and studios among the woods in Branchville, outside Wilton, comprise the only National Park Service site in Connecticut and have been a continuously operating art factory for more than a century.

Art continues to be produced here. Artists Sperry and Doris Andrews have lived in the Weir house since 1957 and still paint. They graciously share their grounds and studio with the public.

But the Andrewses are just one part of a long thread of history made here. The property looks almost as it did when J. Alden Weir bought it in 1882, and there has never been a time since when an artist hasn't resided here. If you wander the grounds, you can see the same landscapes, unmolested by progress, that Weir painted. Weir Farm is fifty miles and fifty billion light years from Manhattan.

The son of a West Point drawing professor, Weir began his career teaching art and painting portraits and still life in New York City. Ironically, he first hated impressionism, faulting it for its rejection of drawing and form. It was after his move to Branchville that Weir began to notice the sunlight and patterns of light, shadow, and color among the woods, gardens, and stone walls in the country. He saw how the grass moved in the wind and how the sky changed tints when a storm picked up. His observations of nature's subtleties caused him to eventually embrace impressionism.

Had you come here in Weir's day, you might have found any of his three daughters (he lost an infant son to diphtheria) riding a family pony or donkey around the farm, and the artist sitting outside at an easel. At times you may have met other painters and friends of Weir such as Childe Hassam, John Twachtman, and John Singer Sargent, all regular visitors.

Weir died in 1919, and daughter Dorothy took over the studio. In the early 1930s Dorothy married Mahonri Young, a talented sculptor and grandson of Mormon leader Brigham Young. It was Mahonri Young who crafted the *This is the Place* monument in Salt Lake City. Young built a studio next to Weir's in order to accommodate that massive work. After Young's death in 1957 his friends Sperry and Doris Andrews purchased the farm.

Guided tours today take you into both the Weir and Young studios. Weir's is a cluttered, barnlike building, used by Sperry Andrews today. Weir generally painted outdoors but would put on finishing touches in the studio.

Young's studio is bigger and more spacious. Though Weir died before this studio was built, some of his artifacts are here, such as a wicker chair in which his wife posed.

Those not taking the guided tour can screen a twenty-minute-long video and examine Weir family photos in the visitor center. There is also a self-guided tour through the surrounding woods taking you to some of Weir's painting sites; a brochure outlining them is on sale for a nominal charge.

You can often see artists and photographers on the premises, inspired by the same parcel of nature that bedazzled Weir. What you won't see here are original completed Weir paintings. To see those, visit the Mattatuck Museum in

Waterbury (Chapter 36), the Wadsworth Athenaeum in Hartford, the Lyman Allyn Art Museum in New London, the Metropolitan Museum of Art and the Brooklyn Museum, both in New York City, and the Phillips Collection in Washington, D.C., for starters.

In addition, a Connecticut Impressionist Art Trail map, highlighting appropriate stops throughout the state, has been developed. Copies are available at Weir Farm or write: Connecticut Impressionist Art Trail, PO Box 793, Old Lyme, CT 06371.

FOR MORE INFORMATION

Location: To get to the Weir Farm National Historic site, take Route 7 to Route 102 to the second left onto Old Branchville Road, then turn left onto Nod Hill Road. The site is at the top of the hill, just past Pelham Lane.

Admission: No charge.

Hours: Daily, April through November; shorter hours December through March.

Contact: Weir Farm National Historic Site, 735 Nod Hill Road, Wilton, CT 06897; (203) 834-1896.

When in the area: There are numerous nature centers in Fairfield County (Chapter 11). There is also the superb Maritime Center at Norwalk (Chapter 9).

Lodging: Ridgefield Motor Inn, 296 Ethan Allen Highway, Ridgefield, CT; (203) 438-3781. West Lane Inn (an 1800s home turned into a country inn), 22 West Lane, Ridgefield, CT; (203) 438-7323. Stonehenge Inn (a country inn well known for its gourmet food offerings), Stonehenge Road, Ridgefield, CT; (203) 438-6511. The Elms Inn (an inn since 1799), 500 Main Street, Ridgefield, CT; (203) 438-2541.

Weir Farm National Historic Site

22

Cajun Country North

THE STORY OF THE CAJUNS OF SOUTH LOUISIANA READS LIKE a Shakespearean tragedy. It tells of exile, pain, heartache, and separation.

Then, why is Cajun music some of the happiest music around, just begging for a party to start? Perhaps it's because celebration is a most satisfying form of preserving a way of life while thumbing one's nose at an unkind past. Life is too short to dwell on misfortunes. *Laissez les bon temps rouler!* is the Cajun cry—"Let the good times roll!"

Every year, in late June and on Labor Day weekend, the little village of Escoheag, Rhode Island, just over the Connecticut border, becomes Cajun country north. In June the Big East Bash takes place. In September it's the Cajun and Bluegrass Festival. The two are separate odes to all things Cajun.

Ever want to sample a taste of alligator? It's on the festival menus, which may also include red beans and rice, étoufées, blackened fish (although that's a Chef Paul Prudhomme creation more than a Cajun tradition), beignets, dirty rice (which gets its label from the chicken liver, pork, and sauces), and gumbo, sort of a bouillabaisse gone berserk. And most anyone who ever heard Hank Williams sing "Jambalaya" will have an urge to try this concoction of beef, ham, or poultry topped by a dark, rich sauce over rice.

But most who come here come for the rhythmic, addictive, exhilarating, insistent beat that is Cajun music. Big names come from their homes in the bayous of southern Louisiana for the Labor Day blowout. The list has included Dewey Balfa, Beausoleil, and D. L. Menard.

The roots of Cajun music, and the Cajuns themselves, are in the North. Cajuns originally were Nova Scotia and New Brunswick Acadians who were exiled in 1763 following the British victory in the French and Indian War. Over time many settled in south Louisiana where "Acadian" gradually became "Cajun." At the festival, it is not uncommon to find a Franco-American from Woonsocket asking performers for the latest news of his cousins living way down yonder in the Louisiana city of Lafayette.

The two festivals are the creations of Providence-based poet and Cajun music lover Franklin Zawacki. The Cajun fest came first, in 1980. Zawacki created it for two reasons: to bring Cajun music to the North and to fill a void for what Zawacki, a single parent, saw as a lack of family events.

He says, "I was distressed. Most activities seemed to be for seniors only or for children only. Cajun music is very inclusive. Grandmas and grandpas dance together; little kids dance with little kids. There is no self-consciousness about age differences."

June's Big Easy fest debuted in 1990 to widen the range of imported music. At this celebration, Tex-Mex and Cajun's urban cousin, zydeco, serenade your ears.

What's the difference between Cajun and zydeco? Says Zawacki, Cajun music clings to tradition. A typical Cajun band is a concoction of fiddle, triangle, electric bass, steel guitar, and accordion. The seemingly insignificant triangle has a major role in Cajun music; it's used to set the beat.

Zydeco features a larger accordion and a washboard instead of a triangle. At one time, an actual washboard was used. Today, it's a "washboard vest," a new instrument developed primarily for zydeco bands. In addition, zydeco has strong African American influences and might include a horn section.

Summer

On festival evenings, dances are held and lessons for novices are given. Amateur musicians bring their own fiddles, accordions, or guitars and join in workshops with the masters. Youngsters can keep busy with crafts such as making a guitar out of a cardboard box.

Richard Naquin of the Louisiana-based Sons of Cajun Heritage credits the tourist interest of the last fifteen years with the revival of all things Cajun.

"We're finally getting recognized," Naquin said. "Many people were embarrassed to speak the Cajun language. But the tourists who come (to Louisiana) like to listen to our music. They like to absorb it. They realize that it's good-time music."

FOR MORE INFORMATION

Location: Escoheag is about one and a half miles over the Connecticut border. From Route 165, take Escoheag Hill Road north to the concert site.

Admission: A fee is charged for the concerts.

Hours: The Big Easy Bash is held the last weekend of June on Saturday and Sunday. The Cajun and Bluegrass Festival takes place every Labor Day weekend, Friday through Sunday.

Contact: Cajun Music, 151 Althea Street, Providence, RI 02907-2801; (401) 351-6312.

Lodging: Best Western West Greenwich Inn, 101 Nooseneck Hill Road (Route 3), West Greenwich, RI; (401) 397-5494. Classic Motor Lodge, 859 Victory Highway (Route 102), West Greenwich, RI; (401) 397-6280. Tamarack Lodge, 10 Rod Road, Voluntown, CT; (860) 376-0224 or (860) 376-0640.

23

Oysters, Quahogs, and Other Assorted Victuals

MIX TWO STATES WITH TONS OF COASTLINE AND YOU HAVE seafood feasts just waiting to happen. Add in some ethnic heritage and you have a full range of gustatory galas.

Following is a lucky seven list of top annual summer food festivals in Connecticut and Rhode Island:

1. Norwalk Seaport Association's Oyster Festival, Connecticut, early September.

   About 100,000 people come to Veterans Park during this three-day gathering, making it one of the largest annual events in Connecticut. Folks can be found perusing the works of more than two hundred juried craftspersons, touring tall ships and antique boats, cruising the harbor, watching the oyster-shucking contest, and did we mention eating oysters on the half shell, fried oysters, and other seafood? Norwalk Seaport Association, 132 Water Street, South Norwalk, CT 06854; (203) 838-9444.

2. Oyster Festival, Milford, Connecticut, third Saturday in August.

   A half-hour drive from Norwalk is Milford, site of a smaller but no less tasty oyster testimonial. From 25,000 to 30,000 people come to Milford's town green and Fowler Field for tastes of oysters, shrimp, clams, grinders, hot dogs, and other foods. There are about 250 craft vendors, environmental booths, a canoe race, and a health fair. Milford Chamber of Commerce, 5 North Broad Street, Milford, CT 06460; (203) 878-0681.

3. Charlestown Seafood Festival, Rhode Island, first Sunday in August.

It is called South County's original seafood festival. Walk around Charlestown's Ninigret Park and you will find approximately fifty food booths offering seafood in all forms, from the conventional to the eccentric. Sample quahogs and crab cakes along with mako shark, calamari, and snail salad. There are also about fifty craft booths, helicopter and carnival rides, and music all day long. Charlestown Chamber of Commerce, PO Box 633, Charlestown, RI 02813; (401) 364-3878.

4. Pasta Challenge, Providence, Rhode Island, early September.

City and regional restaurants serve up the best pasta and sauces in this annual competition. Some of the more unusual entries have been red ale fettucine and chocolate pasta. Cooking demonstrations are scheduled (where observers have picked up tips on making all sorts of pasta, marinara sauce, and grilled pizza). Youngsters can try their hand at crafting necklaces or bracelets from pasta. Keep Providence Beautiful, The Foundry, 235 Promenade Street, Suite #226, Providence, Rhode Island 02908; (401) 351-6440.

5. Bluefish Festival, Clinton, Connecticut, mid-August.

There is something fishy going on annually in this town on Long Island Sound. Every year since 1973, the people of Clinton have served up barrels of bluefish. Nowadays it's most often breaded and baked and served with potatoes and corn.

Festivalgoers can also chow down on scallops, steamers, chowder, lobster, crab, and traditional fair fare such as hot dogs, hamburgers, and cotton candy. Yearly events include a boat parade, usually led by a Coast Guard ship, and the blessing of the fleet. You can browse or buy at a couple dozen craft booths to live music. Peter Moore, 42 Silver Birch Lane, Clinton, CT 06413; (860) 669-0301.

6. Schweppes Great Chowder Cook-Off, Newport, Rhode Island, June.

The origin of chowder has been traced to fishing villages in Brittany, France, where it was called "chaudiere" and was made from fish, vegetables, spices, and ships biscuits. The Miqmak Indians in what is now Atlantic Canada added clams. New Englanders later added milk and anglicized the name as "chowder." Every year in Newport about 5,700 pounds of potatoes, 4,000 pounds of shucked clams, and 3,300 gallons of cream are used as some two dozen restaurants serve up their best chowders. Music, kids' entertainment, and cooking demonstrations supplement the yummy stuff. Newport Yachting Center, 4 Commercial Wharf, PO Box 550, Newport, RI 02840; (401) 846-1600.

7. Johnnycakes on parade, Narragansett, Rhode Island, July.

The South County Museum holds two special events in early July where this distinctly Rhode Island staple is offered. The annual Johnnycake Brunch has three seatings on a July Sunday and always sells out early. On another July Sunday is the museum's antique auto show, where johnnycakes are also served and you do not need to reserve in advance.

And for those who don't know, a johnnycake is sort of a pancake-size fried corn cake, originally introduced to European settlers by Native Americans. It is said that ideal johnnycakes are golden brown on the outside and fluffy inside. The name derives from "journey cake," since they were easy for travelers to carry. South County Museum, PO Box 709, Narragansett, RI 02882-0709; (401) 783-5400.

24

Native American Powwows

MENTION NATIVE AMERICANS, AND THE IMMEDIATE ASSO-
ciation is the land west of us, either the Navajo or Hopi in
the Far West or the Sioux on the Great Plains. The arrival of
the Foxwoods and Mohegan Sun casino/resorts (the subject
of Chapter 51) reminds us that our region has a long Native
American history. Poker chips, however, are not part of
Native American folklore.

Powwows and other cultural events occur throughout
southern New England, most in summer, and all affording a
chance to sample some Native American cuisine and
lifestyle.

Powwows

The Connecticut River Powwow Society, Inc., sponsors a
trio of tribal gatherings. The first is the Strawberry Moon
Festival, taking place the last weekend in June at Four Towns
Fairgrounds in Somers. It commemorates the spring moon
associated with the season of strawberries. The second, the
Connecticut River Powwow, transpires over the last weekend in August at the Polo Grounds in Farmington. The third,
the Pawcatuck-Pequot Powwow, is a fall event, held over
Columbus Day weekend in Highland Orchards Resort Park
in North Stonington. It is a joint effort between the society
and the Pawcatuck Eastern Pequots.

Come to Highland Orchards to witness traditional Native American dancing, storytelling, and craft demonstrations. The Strawberry Moon Powwow is highlighted by a traditional Native American fashion show. Notice the differences between eastern and western Indian dress. At one powwow, an Iroquois from New York state stressed how his headdress consisted of a single feather, much more basic than the expansive headdress worn by Apache dancers from Arizona.

Also expect intertwining with modern times. Society spokesperson Elaine Alson says, "Some Native Americans show up in traditional regalia, while others go into the circle wearing sneakers, jeans, and jackets. We insist that all crafts are made by Native Americans, but some are coming out with modern designs. We want people to know that Native Americans are working in factories, or in entertainment, or have office jobs. Native Americans are doctors and lawyers. They are no different than anyone else."

Delicacies for sale must be derived from Native American foods, such as wild rice, corn, venison, rabbit, buffalo, and fry breads. You might, therefore, be able to indulge in an Indian taco, or buffalo sausages and buffalo burgers, as opposed to hot dogs and hamburgs. Then again, you may have the chance to taste the truly traditional Native American Three Sisters rice dish; the three sisters are corn, beans, and squash, all served over wild rice.

Contact: Connecticut River Powwow Society, Inc., c/o Richard Harris, 118 Ingham Hill Road, Old Saybrook, CT 06475; (203) 684-6984.

Admission: A fee is charged.

Quinnehtukqut Rendezvous and Native American Festival

This event is a combined celebration of Native Americans (the festival) and early European settlers (the rendezvous).

One can visit both a Native American village and a pioneer settlement. You might be able to explore a re-created wigwam, a conical shelter of white poplar bark that was home to eastern Native Americans, or a wickiup, a hut in the shape of a pyramid and made from cattail reeds.

As at the powwows, dancers from both eastern and western tribes can be present, and crafts from several tribes are for sale. The event takes place in early August at Haddam Meadows State Park along the banks of the Connecticut River. (*Quinnehtukqut* is an Algonquian word roughly translated as "the land of the long, tidal river." You can see how it evolved into a certain state's name.)

Contact: Cathie Condio, CFC Associates, 19 Blinn Street, East Hartford, CT 06108; (860) 282-1404.

Admission: A fee is charged.

Narragansett Annual August Meeting

In what is now Rhode Island, the Narragansett Indian Tribe held its first annual meeting a century or two before European settlers arrived. One Narragansett spokesman said, "This meeting is the continuation of living history that predates any colonial contact."

The two-day gathering commences with the cleansing of the circle by the tribal medicine man and includes singing, dancing, crafts making, and food. Some victuals have a distinct Rhode Island flavor; johnnycakes and dishes made with clams and quahogs are commonly on the menu.

Contact: Chief and Council, Narragansett Indian Tribe, PO Box 268, Charlestown, RI 02813; (401) 364-1100 or (401) 364-9832.

Admission: A fee is charged.

25

Jamestown Island

JAMESTOWN IS NEWPORT LITE. OFFICIALLY KNOWN AS Conanicut Island, Jamestown is coastal Rhode Island without glitziness and ritziness. Don't come here for mansions or packaged tourist attractions. There are museums on this seafaring island, but they are loose ships. Their hours are limited, and the displays are homespun, not state of the art.

Do come here to get a real taste of summertime on a Rhode Island island. This island is not deserted, but the thrust of tourists drive not to, but *through*, Jamestown on their way to the toll bridge to Newport.

"It's either rural and quiet or boring, depending how you look at it," says Lee Howard, executive director of the Jamestown Village Corporation.

The prettiest spot on this island in Narragansett Bay might be Beavertail State Park. At the island's southernmost tip, the park hosts surf fishermen and painters who stand among the rocks as the Atlantic crashes onto the land and seagulls sing their summer songs while a breeze soothes your skin.

But this plaudit to peacefulness is also a menace to mariners. The waters here have always been treacherous. A posted marker at the state park describes how Beavertail Point has been a site of shipwrecks since colonial times. In order to reduce the number of shipwrecks in the 1800s, the point was a testing area for signaling devices to guide sailors on foggy nights.

Then there is the traditional way of guiding mariners—a lighthouse. The one here and the former lighthouse-keeper's home next to it have been transformed into a museum. Step inside to see models of lighthouses, classic photos, and an old lighthouse light.

The outside is as much of a museum as the interior. Scattered around the structure are informational markers informing us about topics from marine life to ocean vessels. One identifies eleven boats of the bay, coded with illustrations. A quick read and you will be able to peg that sturdy, flat-bottomed boat out in the water as a quahog skiff. Another marker describes how blue mussels anchor themselves to rocks with flexible threads, keeping themselves from being washed away at high tide. Pretty clever for a creature not known for its brain size.

The one town on the island, Jamestown, is relaxing, natural, and relatively free of Hawaiian shirt–wearing tourists with Instamatics. This is a real seaside community, supporting a library, churches, a recreation center (with public rest rooms), and a marina as well as two small museums. One, the Fire Department Memorial Museum, has an 1894 steam engine and antique fire-fighting equipment. The other, the Jamestown Museum, is heavy on hands-on maritime memorabilia. (Bang a gong. Ring a bell. Try on a hat.) It also has material relating to the ferry that sailed regularly from here to Newport until the Newport Bridge rendered it obsolete in 1969.

Markers at the town dock display old photos of the ferry, too, and don't neglect to examine the likenesses of old ferry tickets, also embedded in a marker. This is a fine place for an ice-cream cone, a leisurely walk, or a photo opportunity: the Newport Bridge, at times, seems to disappear right into the fog.

North of the town along North Road, right in the heart of the island, is one of the last remaining colonial windmills in New England. Constructed in 1787, it was used throughout the 1800s and is open to the public today. Also on North Road is Watson Farm, operated as a working farm and a property of the Society for the Preservation of New England Antiquities. A self-guided walking tour takes visitors through the barnyard, along the beach, and through an old orchard, home to animals ranging from deer to butterflies.

If the only exercise you wish to do is turn over every half hour to avoid sunburn, take note that the island has one public beach, Mackerel Cove Town Beach on Beavertail Road. Daily admission is steep—$10 as we went to press—so, plan on a full day's visit if you want your money's worth.

To combine recreation with history, visit the remnants of either of two forts. Fort Wetherill State Park has more fortifications than Fort Getty Recreational Area, but Fort Getty has overnight camping. Fort Wetherill, however, is home to some of the best diving on the East Coast.

Some of the best shopping opportunities take place in early August. An annual art show is held on the first August weekend, a craft show the second.

FOR MORE INFORMATION

Location: Jamestown Island sits in Narragansett Bay between Newport and the mainland. From the mainland, take Jamestown Bridge (Route 138 heading east). From Newport, take Newport Bridge (Route 138 heading west).
Hours: All the listed attractions have limited hours, which can change according to staffing. As we went to press, all kept some sort of weekend hours, with the exception of the Fire Department Memorial Museum. (Watson Farm is closed Saturday.) Call or write ahead if you have your heart set on seeing any particular attraction.
Contact: Jamestown Village Association, PO Box 35, Jamestown, RI 02835; (401) 423-3650.

Lodging: Bay Voyage Inn (a former Gilded Age hotel), 150 Conanicus Avenue, Jamestown, RI; (800) 225-3522 or (401) 847-9780. Jamestown B and B, 59 Walcott Avenue, Jamestown, RI; (401) 423-1338. Lionel Champlin House (B and B), 20 Lincoln Street, Jamestown, RI; (401) 423-2782. East Bay B and B, 14 Union Street, Jamestown, RI; (401) 423-2715.

Summer

26

Skyrockets and Parades

TWO CENTURIES AGO IN BRISTOL, RHODE ISLAND, Independence Day might have been celebrated with a colonial musket. Today it's celebrated with a bang—make that many bangs—part of a fireworks display from a barge in Bristol Harbor. It is one of two long-standing July 4th parades in the state.

The obligatory fireworks are just a supplement to the main July 4 celebration in Bristol, a roughly three-hour-long assembly of floats, antique fire engines, marching bands, horses, mounted police color guards, and a few rhinestone-bedecked, fine-feathered Mummers bands direct from Philadelphia. In the harbor there is always a visiting navy ship available for boarding, a tradition since 1976 when the USS *Juniata* made a stop here.

The Bristol fest is said to be the oldest Fourth of July celebration in the country, dating to 1785. It's also one of the biggest, at least for a town of 21,600. People begin staking out parade-watching spots before dawn, and by the time the first marching steps are heard at the corner of Hope Street (Route 114) and Chestnut Street at 10:30 A.M., there are likely 200,000 people in attendance.

Some advice for those coming from out of town:

1. Try to be in the center of Bristol no later than 8 A.M. Traffic can be gridlocked by 8:30.

107

2. You will hear the most band music if you are near the reviewing stand at the town common on High Street between Church and State Streets. Arrive in Bristol earlier than 8 A.M. if you want a much envied locale by the reviewing stand.

3. Look for colored bands posted high up on telephone poles. At least one-third of the marching bands are instructed to play in the vicinity of the color-coded bands. Post yourself by one and you will be certain to hear one-third of the music.

4. Those who attended the parade a decade ago might remember rowdiness associated with alcohol-saturated partyers. In 1988 nine bands sent letters saying they would quit the parade if the crowds weren't better controlled. The parade route was then declared an alcohol-free zone, and the problem has been relegated to the past.

Arrive in town prior to the night of July 3 and you are invited to attend the annual fife-and-drum-corps competition at Mount Hope High School on Chestnut Street. The various corps can be seen marching down Hope Street during the parade the next morning.

Following the parade is a carnival on the town common, and later that night the scintillated skies above Bristol let you know that the fireworks show has begun.

The Arnold Mills Parade in Cumberland is a July 4 parade for wise guys. It is officially an "ancient and horribles" parade, filled with satire and sarcasm, with its roots in the nation's 1926 sesquicentennial. Over the last decade or two, floats and marching bands have taken the form of the eight-foot-long ant that once resided at Three Mile Island, the Donald Trump "Save the Donald" telethon crew, the Olympic crap-shooting team, the Bill and Hillary White-

Summer

water bailout staff, and the Jim and Tammy Faye Bakker rescue crew, hauling a wagon labeled "Tammy Faye's makeup."

Parade organizer Steve Macauley says, "It helps to look at things through a comic eye. Life needs to be turned upside down sometimes. Our participation in the parade is something we look forward to each year. We are never at a loss for material."

From the ridiculous to the sublime, the parade also has its share of traditional marching bands, Shriners in their miniature cars, and oddities such as bicyclists peddling down Nate Whipple Highway on high-wheelers or unicycles.

Many of the sights worth examining aren't in the parade at all; they are the many historic buildings along the route. Near the beginning are the two-and-one-half-story Colonial Cottage, also known as the Captain John Walcott House, and the Greek Revival–style William A. Walcott House, built in 1838. Closer to the end of the route is the Arnold Mills Methodist Church, a Federal-style house of worship dedicated in 1827.

The church grounds are the setting as well for a concert with music usually provided by the Rhode Island Veterans Band. Also on the slate is a four-mile-long road race. Its starting line is at the Lafayette Masonic Temple.

For More Information

Contact: Fourth of July Committee, PO Box 561, Bristol, RI 02809; (401) 253-9461. Arnold Mills Parade Association, PO Box 7473, Cumberland, RI 02864; (401) 658-1502.

Skyrockets and Parades

Fall

27

The Festivals of Fall

AUTUMN IS THE TIME OF YEAR WHEN NEW ENGLAND celebrates its colors: red as in apples; orange as in autumn leaves; white as in the first frost; green as in crisp, fresh currency.

It is now when nature and mankind both show off their best crafted works. Nature's are temporary, but free for the viewing. Mankind's are more permanent, but cost. But what you pay for are some of the best-made handcrafts in New England. Christmas and Hanukkah are not far away, and these fairs are prime places to find holiday gifts that did not roll off an assembly line in Taipei.

Following are some of the most long-standing and respected fall crafts and harvest fairs in our region:

Cornwall, Connecticut—Mohawk Mountain Fall Foliage Craft Fair   The biggest thrills are round-trip rides up chair lifts for a skier's eye view of the autumn vibrancy. There are usually about forty craftspersons in addition to kids' activities such as hayrides or fire-engine rides and face painting. Late October; there is a charge for chairlift rides, but no general admission. (860) 672-6100.

Cranston, Rhode Island—Cranston Historical Society Arts & Crafts Show   On the grounds of the society's Sprague Mansion, built in 1790, about seventy-five craftspersons gather for two days. You can tour the mansion and grab a cup of tea or slice of pastry at Mabel's Tea House, operated by mansion caretaker Mabel Kelley. Early October; free, donation requested for mansion tours. (401) 944-9226 or (401) 781-0521.

Danielson, Connecticut—Outdoor Arts and Crafts Festival What better setting for a fall fest than this—approximately eighty exhibitors selling their wares around a gazebo on the village green.

About 15 percent are artists selling oils or pen-and-ink sketches. Musicians, ranging from a jazz combo to a classical harpist, have been known to serenade arts-and-crafts lovers from the gazebo during this two-day event. Late September; free. (860) 774-4377.

Glastonbury, Connecticut—Apple Harvest Festival Upwards of 3,000 apple pies are sold, and between 20,000 and 25,000 people annually attend this weekend-long festival. There are usually more than a hundred craft exhibitors, along with a parade, face painting, storytelling, and square dancing. Mid-October; free. (860) 659-3587.

Johnston, Rhode Island—Apple Festival Apples are the dominant theme here, too: apple pies, apple cider, candy apples, apple tarts, for example. There are also standard staples such as clam cakes (standard, at least, for Rhode Island), chowder, and hot dogs. One annual event is the apple pie bake-off. About fifty craftspersons sell their wares, mostly handmade. Late September; free. (401) 273-1310.

Ledyard, Connecticut—Colonial Crafts Festival The emphasis here is on colonial-period demonstrations, and you can buy some products made by the spinner, potter, tinsmith, broom maker, or perhaps furniture maker. All crafts are made using colonial-era methods. The fest takes place in and outside of the Nathan Lester House and Farm Tool Museum. Musical entertainment may be provided by a fife-and-drum corps or a fiddler, there is often an encampment, and children can try their hand at making potpourri or a quill pen. Late September; admission charge. (860) 464-1865.

Middletown, Rhode Island—Norman Bird Sanctuary Harvest Fair For two days there is some real wild life here. Folks fight with pillows atop a log balanced over a mud pit or ascend to the top of a Crisco-caked greased pole. On the mild side, there are about four dozen New England artisans selling their wares alongside scarecrow-making and bird-of-prey demonstrations. This is one event in Newport County's monthlong Harvest-by-the-Sea Celebration (see subsequent Newport listing). Early October; admission charge. (401) 846-2577.

Narragansett, Rhode Island—South County Museum Harvest Festival & Apple Pie Contest For one Sunday in October, the scents of hot apple pie fill the seaside air. Like any other good Rhode Island fest, this one also has clam cakes, johnnycakes, and chowder. There are also a scarecrow-making contest, hayrides, forty or so craftspersons, and demonstrations of arts such as spinning, rug making, cider pressing, and blacksmithing. Early October; free. (401) 783-5400.

Newport, Rhode Island—Harvest By the Sea This "harvest" is an umbrella title for a cornucopia of harvests taking place throughout October. Commonly included are the Norman Bird Sanctuary Harvest Fair (see prior Middletown listing), the "Harvest Weekend Extravaganza" in downtown Newport, an Oktoberfest and the "Taste of Rhode Island" at the Newport Yachting Center, farmers markets, hayrides, and culinary lessons. Admission charge for most events. (800) 326-6030 or (401) 849-8048.

The Festivals of Fall

Norwich, Connecticut—Harvest Festival of Crafts The sixty or so craft sellers are indoors in the Norwichtown Mall in the historic district of Norwich. The hayrides and face painting take place outdoors on the mall grounds. Consider supplementing the fair with an autumn walk through the historic Old Burying Ground and Norwichtown Green. Mid-October, free. (860) 442-7976.

Stamford, Connecticut—Harvest Fair Taking place at the Stamford Museum & Nature Center, this one-day fair is another place to go for those who want to watch crafts made from scratch. Craft demonstrators could include a tinsmith, farrier, blacksmith, potter, or glassblower. Visitors can try their hand at making crafts, and there is special entertainment for children. Late September; admission charge. (203) 322-1646.

Woodbury, Connecticut—Fall Festival A true hands-on event, this festival is held at Flanders Nature Center. Activities have included leaf rubbing, hayrides, knot tying, pumpkin carving, apple bobbing, and guided nature walks. Crafts are made (and sold) on the premises, and rare birds or other animals are exhibited. Late September or early October; admission charge. (203) 263-3711.

28

The Artists of Old Lyme

IF YOUR PARENTS EVER TOLD YOU NOT TO DRAW ON THE walls at home, suspend that thought when you walk through the Florence Griswold Museum in Old Lyme. It was in this house that the American impressionist movement thrived and where it was a mark of honor to be asked to draw on the walls.

The story behind the artists' colony here goes like this: Born and raised in this late-Georgian-style mansion built in 1817, Griswold was the daughter of a packet ship captain who lost his fortune with the advent of the steamship in the 1860s. When Florence's mother died in 1899, Florence came into possession of the once glorious mansion. Since she had no money to keep it up, she began taking in boarders.

That year American landscape painter Henry Ward Ranger came from Paris to Old Lyme and rented a room in the home. Ranger, a disciple of the murky, dark French Barbizon school of landscape painting, was attracted by the area's rocky pastures, salt meadows, and tidal rivers. Knowing how pleased Ranger was with his accommodations, other artists followed him, the most famous being Childe Hassam. But Hassam rejected Ranger's Barbizon look for the brighter French impressionistic style, the same style that J. Alden Weir was celebrating farther west in Wilton (see Chapter 21).

Florence Griswold was a hospitable host, letting her artist boarders stay for not much in return. It is said that the artists became a second family, and the group was known as Miss Florence and her "boys" (although there were some "girls" in residence, too, including Matilda Browne and Bessie Vonnoh). If the American impressionist movement was born at the farm of J. Alden Weir, it was here that it grew and prospered.

Florence Griswold died in 1937, and the museum was opened ten years later. There are two main features that make this art museum different from others: (1) it is located in a mansion that still looks like a home; and (2) the best works of art are painted directly on walls and doors as well as hanging in frames.

Only the most highly regarded of Miss Florence's guests were invited to decorate a door or wall. On one door in the front parlor is the pastoral *Monarch of the Farm*, an oil depiction of a cow resting in a barn, by Will Howe.

The dining room is filled with door and wall art, and the one that grabs most visitors' attention is *The Fox Hunt*, drawn by Henry Rankin Poore in 1901 and 1902. The mural over the mantel is a caricature featuring twenty-four members of the colony. Childe Hassam, known for shocking the community occasionally, is painting bare-chested, risqué in those times even for a man, and an embarrassed Matilda Browne is depicted throwing her arms up in horror. Meanwhile, Henry Ward Ranger, of the old Barbizon school, runs after artists chasing the popular Hassam.

Common canvas paintings hang here, too. The most popular might be William Chadwick's *On the Porch*, in which a pretty young woman in flower-topped hat sits at a rectangular table on the Griswold House side porch. Verdant vines weave in and out of the trellises, with a floral mass of purple and blue in the background.

Where were such masterworks crafted? Have a look inside Chadwick's studio, where he painted from around 1920 until he died in 1962. It's in back of the house, and it looks just as if Chadwick only left it to go for a walk.

Fall

Two nearby galleries feature temporary exhibits. Next door to the Griswold Museum is the gallery of the Lyme Art Association, open since 1921. Exhibitions have included art by association members and children as well as retrospective shows celebrating the group's founding artists.

Down the road is the Lyme Academy of Fine Arts. Housed in an 1817 Federal-period home and founded in 1976, the academy hosts shows and offers art classes, with an emphasis on the classes. There is a two-room gallery for exhibitions, usually works of area artists or academy students or faculty.

FOR MORE INFORMATION

Location: All three museums are located on Lyme Street in Old Lyme, off Interstate 95, exit 70.

Admission: A fee is charged for the Florence Griswold Museum. Donations are requested for the Lyme Art Association and the Lyme Academy of Fine Arts.

Hours: The Florence Griswold Museum is open Tuesday through Saturday, and Sunday afternoon, June through November; Wednesday through Saturday and Sunday afternoon the rest of the year. Chadwick's studio is open May through October. The Lyme Art Association is open Tuesday through Saturday and Sunday afternoon, May through December; varied hours the rest of the year. The Lyme Academy of Fine Arts is open Tuesday through Saturday and Sunday afternoon.

Contact: Florence Griswold Museum, 96 Lyme Street, Old Lyme, CT 06371; (860) 434-5542. Lyme Art Association, 90 Lyme Street, Old Lyme, CT 06371; (860) 434-7802. Lyme Academy of Fine Arts, 84 Lyme Street, Old Lyme, CT 06371; (860) 434-5232.

When in the area: To the west are the art (and other) museums of Yale University in New Haven (Chapter 46). To

The Artists of Old Lyme

the east is New London, home of the U.S. Coast Guard Academy (Chapter 2).

Lodging: Bayberry Motor Inn, 436 Shore Road, Old Lyme, CT; (860) 434-3024. Comfort Inn, 100 Essex Road, Old Saybrook, CT; (860) 395-1414. Old Saybrook Motor Hotel, 7 North Main Street, Old Saybrook, CT; (860) 388-3463. Old Lyme Inn (a Victorian-era B and B), 85 Lyme Street, Old Lyme, CT; (800) 434-5352 or (860) 434-2600. Bee & Thistle Inn (a B and B built as a private home in 1756), 100 Lyme Street, Old Lyme, CT 06371; (800) 622-4946 or (860) 434-1667.

Fall

29

Taste the Wine

THE NAPA VALLEY OF CALIFORNIA AND THE FINGER LAKES region of New York might grab all the publicity, but here in southern New England we can see our own places where the wine flows like water. To many people, even among those who live in Connecticut or Rhode Island, that's news.

"Over 50 percent of the people who visit were surprised to hear that there is a winery in Connecticut," admits Edmee DeWitt of Chamard Wineries in Clinton, Connecticut. "I can't believe you grow grapes here," is a common response.

Actually, the natural air-conditioning created by Long Island Sound and the Atlantic Ocean provides prime conditions for growing grapes. In addition, adds DeWitt, "We are at about the same latitude as France's Bordeaux region. Many people don't realize that."

Susan Samson of Sakonnet Vineyards in Little Compton, Rhode Island, adds that the local climes might be ideal for wine making, but the nuances are pure New England. "Our property is surrounded by rock walls, which have been here since this land was originally farmed."

Chamard and Sakonnet are among enterprises offering tours of their facilities along with wine tasting. And what's the proper way to taste the wine? True connoisseurs follow four steps: swirl, sniff, sip, spit. But the overwhelming majority of visitors to southern New England's wineries are not connoisseurs and know as much about the finer points of wine tasting as they do about microphysics. At Chamard wineries there is a bucket for spitting, but most visitors swallow the wine. And that's just fine. Says DeWitt, "We say, 'You have your own palate. We don't tell you what to like and what not to like. It's up to you.'"

Samson advises, "Don't be scared to ask questions. People are afraid to look stupid. But always ask what kind of food you serve with this wine, or whether it needs to be chilled."

She adds, "Wine is not a mystery like some people make it out to be. Either you like it or you don't. A friend of mine describes wines as either 'yuck' or 'yum.'"

Consider these wineries for your next tasting trip, and decide what you think is "yuck" or "yum":

Bishop Farms Winery 500 South Meriden Road, Cheshire, CT 06410; (203) 272-8243. The specialties at this sizable farm store are the fruit wines, including apple, apple-cranberry, apple-raspberry, apple-blueberry, and blueberry. A few grape wines are sold but are not produced here. No tours; tasting only.

Chamard Vineyards 115 Cow Hill Road, Clinton, CT 06413; (860) 664-0299. About 80 percent of Chamard's wines are chardonnays. You will also find cabernet sauvignon, pinot noir, merlot, and cabernet franc. Full winery tours take twenty to twenty-five minutes. Note that Chamard harvests its grapes by utilizing a computerized pneumatic press to gently squeeze juice from the picked fruit. Visitors often buy wine here and picnic at nearby Hammonnasset State Park.

Diamond Hill Vineyards 3145 Diamond Hill Road, Cumberland, Rhode Island; (800) 752-2505 or (401) 333-2751. "Our baby is pinot noir," says co-owner Claire Berntson.

Diamond Hill also produces dry, semidry, and dessert fruit wines from blueberries, peaches, and apples. Berntson says, "We want to show that fruit wines do not have to be only sweet dessert wines." Half-hour tours take place on Sundays, but you can taste on any afternoon except Tuesday.

DiGrazia Vineyards, Ltd. 131 Tower Road, Brookfield, CT 06804; (203) 775-1616. Obstetrician/gynecologist Paul DeGrazia gave birth to DiGrazia Vineyards in 1978, and the first four brands of wine were released six years later. Today there are about thirty wine products, including autumn spice made from white grapes, sugar pumpkins, and spices; and honey blush, with honey used in place of preservatives. Tours are Wednesday through Sunday, May through December; weekends only the rest of the year.

Haight Vineyard 29 Chestnut Hill Road, Litchfield, CT 06759; (800) 325-5567 (in Connecticut) or (860) 567-4045. Also at Olde Mystic Village, Mystic, CT 06355; (800) 582-7624 (in Connecticut) or (860) 572-1978. The winery was established in Litchfield in 1978, and in 1983 its first sparkling wine was released. In 1990 the Mystic location opened so chardonnay and Riesling grapes could be grown in a friendlier climate than that of colder Litchfield. Tours are offered at both venues. Litchfield has picnic tables, while Mystic has a museum-style "Wine Education Center."

Heritage Vineyards 291 North Burnham Highway, Lisbon, CT 06351; (860) 376-0659. A recent entry into the field, clinical psychologist Diane Powell began pressing grapes in 1994. As Powell is a northern California native, perhaps the fruit of the vine is in her blood: in her first year of pressing, she won a bronze medal for her chardonnay in the Con-

Taste the Wine

necticut Amateur Wine Competition. Short guided tours are offered Friday through Sunday from Memorial Day through December. (860) 376-0659.

Hopkins Vineyard Hopkins Road, New Preston, CT 06777; (860) 868-7954. The Hopkins family began farming here in 1787, and their descendents opened the vineyard in 1979. About a dozen wines of all sorts are produced in a renovated 19th-century barn. Self-guided tours only. Hours are daily from May through December; Friday through Sunday the rest of the year.

Newport Vineyards 909 East Main Street, Middletown, RI 02840; (401) 848-5161. In 1977 U.S. Navy captain Richard Alexander wanted to put his twenty acres of land just north of Newport to agricultural use. He chose to plant grapes and served up wines until he retired from wine making in December 1995. Current owner John Nunes Jr. produces eight wines: five whites, a blush, a red table wine, and a port dry. Guided tours take about twenty minutes and include looks at the fermentation tanks, the oak aging room, and the hand-operated bottling area. Tours daily, year-round.

Nutmeg Vineyard 800 Bunker Hill Road, Coventry, CT (mailing address: PO Box 146, Andover, CT 06232); (860) 742-8402. Operating one of the smaller regional wineries, the Nutmeg staff hopes to grow but admits, "Bigness is not one of our goals." Production is limited to fewer than 1,000 cases per year. The wine list has seven entries, ranging from a dry, white seyval blanc to a medium-sweet raspberry. Visitors can tour and taste on weekends, year-round.

Sakonnet Vineyards 162 West Main Road, PO Box 197, Little Compton, RI 02837; (401) 635-8486. Lolly and Jim Mitchell founded Sakonnet in 1975, but it has been in the hands of Earl and Susan Samson since 1987. On forty-five acres they produce eleven wines, including chardonnay, Vidal blanc, and cabernet Franc. With a nod to the famous yacht races that once passed Sakonnet Point, the Samsons have named two of their own blends America's Cup Red and Spinnaker White. Guided tours, including a fifteen-minute slide show, are offered year-round, Wednesday through Sunday; wine tasting is daily, and picnics are encouraged.

Taste the Wine

30

Fall Meanderings

DON'T THINK FOR A MINUTE THAT NORTHERN NEW ENGLAND has a monopoly on the fairest of fall foliage. Here in southern New England we have maples and ponds and stone fences and white-steepled churches—everything that makes New England look just as it should look.

On top of that we have some surprises, such as a candy-colored mansion and a library with a fluted Spanish tile roof that might seem more at home in Santa Barbara.

You can ramble along any back roads in southern New England and encounter the best colors fall has to offer. However, two routes we recommend will take you to Connecticut's northern corners, to the foothills of the Berkshires in the northwest and the countryside of the northeast.

Northeast

First, to the northeast. It is not as well traveled as the Litchfield Hills farther west, which some may see as a plus. But it is also not as hilly, and some people say scenery is nothing without a view of a color-packed hill. The lack of traffic versus the lack of hills—it's a trade-off.

What you do have in northeastern Connecticut are villages such as Woodstock, but there are no mud-caked concertgoers in this Woodstock. Here you will find the peach-colored Roseland Cottage, a quirky home filled with gables and angles. Built in 1846 as the summer retreat for a businessman named Henry C. Bowen, it is open to the public.

The cottage faces Woodstock's pristine town green; also facing it are the white-steepled First Congregational Church and the Woodstock Academy, founded in 1801. Every September the town is also home to an influx of horses and cattle, when the Woodstock Fair comes to town.

From here the choice is yours. You can head west along Route 171 toward the community of Union and Bigelow Hollow State Park, a prime picnic spot. Along the winding and narrow two-lane road you will be bordered by farms and barns, woods, and stone fences.

The other option is to travel south on Route 169, through South Woodstock and thick forest, to Pomfret. Like Woodstock, Pomfret is home to a private school, the Pomfret Academy. The campus's Clark Memorial Chapel appears as if it would be more at home along the Moselle River in Germany—it's a medieval-styled building that screams for attention.

From here consider taking Route 169 to Route 101 east through the industrial and definitely "unscenic" heart of Dayville, then under Interstate 395 to the Rhode Island border. Hugging the state line is Jerimoth Hill, Rhode Island's highest point at 812 feet above sea level. (OK, so it's not Mount Whitney—after all, this is Rhode Island.) At North Foster, head north about six miles on Route 94 until it ends at the junction of Route 44. Head east for a possible picnic or walk at George Washington Management Area, or west to return to Connecticut.

Northwest

The definition of the Litchfield Hills depends on where you call home. If you live in Manhattan, they are a quick, bucolic getaway. If you live in Vermont, they are an industrial state's lame attempt at country. If you live in Connecticut, they are the most famous destination for those seeking a rural getaway.

Regardless, Litchfield is a small town gem that the National Park Service described as "probably New England's finest surviving example of a typical late-18th-century New England town." (Take that, Vermont!)

The center of Litchfield is on the National Register of Historic Places, and the Congregational Church, with its sky-piercing steeple, is said to be one of New England's most photographed. The Tapping Reeve House and Law School, established in 1774 as the first law school in the country, is open to the public. One of its first students was the notorious Aaron Burr, brother-in-law of the founder, Judge Tapping Reeve.

You can also check out the Litchfield Historical Society museum for looks at Early American art and furniture, White Flower Farm, with eight acres of display gardens and a retail garden store, and White Memorial Conservation Center Museum, with a nature trail and exhibits. Then there is the White Memorial Foundation, the state's largest nature center and wildlife sanctuary, with thirty-five miles of hiking trails.

Take Route 63 north six miles to Goshen, a little less polished than Litchfield and therefore, some might say, a little more real. Goshen has its own historical society, with old clocks, paintings, and tools. A left onto Route 4 will take you through Mohawk Mountain State Forest, a welcoming place to unpack the picnic basket and see the leaves up close. Then head north on Route 7. In West Cornwall is one of the last remaining covered bridges in the state.

You can continue your trip by paralleling the Housatonic River along Route 7. In Canaan, take Route 44 east to Haystack Mountain State Park and the center of Norfolk. Whitehouse, the colonial white mansion facing the triangular village green, is the main building of Yale University's Summer School of Music.

The building with the Spanish tile roof is Norfolk's library. Not very "New England," is it? But check out the 19th-century-style directional signs on the green across from Whitehouse. Town names are embellished with images of wild rabbit and deer. This should make you feel more at home.

FOR MORE INFORMATION

Location: Roseland Cottage is on Route 169 facing the common in Woodstock.

Admission: A fee is charged.

Hours: June through mid-October, Wednesday through Sunday, late morning through afternoon.

Contact: Roseland Cottage, (860) 928-4074.

Lodging: Inn at Woodstock Hill (a restored country estate), 94 Plaine Hill Road, South Woodstock, CT; (860) 928-0528. Beaver Pond B and B (a small country B and B), 68 Cutler Hill Road, Woodstock, CT; (860) 974-3312. Karinn (a historic inn), 330 Pomfret Street (Routes 44 and 169), Pomfret Center, CT; (860) 928-5492. King's Inn (a motel), 5 Heritage Road, Putnam, CT; (800) 541-7304 or (860) 928-7961.

Location: Litchfield Historical Society Museum and the Tapping Reeve House and Law School are on South Street facing the green. White Flower Farm is on Route 63, three and a half miles south of the center of town. White Memorial Conservation Center Museum and White Memorial Foundation are on Route 202, two miles west of town. Goshen Historical Society is on Route 63 in the center of the village.

Admission: A fee is charged for Litchfield Historical Society Museum, Tapping Reeve House and Law School, and

White Memorial Conservation Center Museum. Admission is free for White Flower Farm and White Memorial Foundation.

Hours: Litchfield Historical Society Museum is open mid-April through mid-November, Tuesday through Saturday, and Sunday afternoon. Tapping Reeve House & Law School is open mid-May through mid-October, Tuesday through Saturday, and Sunday afternoon. White Flower Farm is open April through late December. White Memorial Conservation Center Museum is open year-round, Monday through Saturday, and Sunday afternoon. White Memorial Foundation grounds are open year-round, daily. Goshen Historical Society is open year-round by appointment only.

Contact: Litchfield Historical Society Museum and Tapping Reeve House and Law School, (860) 567-4501. White Flower Farm, (860) 567-8789. White Memorial Conservation Center Museum and White Memorial Foundation, (860) 567-0857. Goshen Historical Society, (860) 491-9610.

Lodging: Litchfield Inn (a country inn), Route 202, Litchfield, CT; (800) 499-3444 or (860) 567-4503. Tollgate Hill Inn (built as a way station in 1745), Route 202 at Tollgate Road, Litchfield, CT; (800) 445-3903 or (860) 567-4545. Mountain View Inn (a Victorian country inn), Route 272, Norfolk, CT; (860) 542-6991. Cornwall Inn (a former 19th-century inn), 270 Kent Road (Route 7), Cornwall Bridge, CT; (800) 786-6884 or (860) 672-6884. Hitching Post Country Motel, 45 Kent Road (Route 7), Cornwall Bridge, CT; (860) 672-6219.

Fall Meanderings

31

Museum of American Political Life

"WE DON'T WANT ELEANOR EITHER"

So reads the message on a political campaign button dating to one of Franklin Roosevelt's reelection campaigns more than a half century ago. Some Republicans were tired of what they considered to be radical ideas of the Democratic president and the pushiness of his overbearing wife. Some went so far as to claim that Eleanor really wore the pants in the White House.

So, here we are in the 1990s. What else is new?

The button is one of hundreds displayed at the Museum of American Political Life on the campus of the University of Hartford in West Hartford, Connecticut. What better time to visit than fall, the conventional time of heavy campaigning and politicking?

Most buttons and other political ephemera—George Washington's inaugural buttons made of copper and brass, a license plate reading AUH2O (the chemical symbols for gold and water), a tin parade lantern used in 1840 by supporters of Henry Clay, and an organically made "McGovern Muffin," to name just four—are displayed as part of the History Wall, a seventy-foot-long display case and accompanying time line covering the museum's full east wall.

The History Wall tells the story of each presidential campaign, connecting the administrations of George Washington and Bill Clinton. Posted along with the political news and mementos of each election year are listings of events and trends from the nonpolitical world. For example, as we pore over relics from the Ulysses S. Grant presidency, we read that the first Kentucky Derby took place at the same time. While admiring a JFK lapel button we read about Warhol's soup cans, Updike's *Rabbit Run*, and the introduction of The Pill.

Dominating the museum is a life-size reproduction of a 19th-century torchlight parade. The marchers, often thousands at one time, carried flaming torches and were commonly followed by a marching band, fire-fighting apparatus, and fireworks wagons. At the center of the parade was the candidate.

The museum's torchlight parade covers two floors, beginning on the entrance level, extending onto a staircase and winding down to the main floor. It includes seventeen life-size mannequins in whose hands are political signs, banners, and torches. In the front of the parade is a bow-tied and vest-wearing 19th-century politico, one arm raised, the other clasped to his heart, imploring voters to support his candidacy.

The age of television is not ignored here. In one gallery visitors watch videotaped excerpts of defining political moments on the tube. There are, for instance, snippets and analysis of the 1960 Kennedy-Nixon debate and Richard Nixon's Checkers speech. There is an "Ike for President" cartoon ad and a thirty-minute political promotional program called "Coffee with the Kennedys."

Why is this, one of the country's premier museums of politics, situated in West Hartford? The *true* reason is that the core of the museum collection—40,000 pieces of political memorabilia—was donated by J. Doyle DeWitt, a long-time executive with Travelers Insurance who spent four decades amassing his own multitude of political memorabilia. (Today there are well in excess of 60,000 items in the museum collection, only a small fraction of which are on view.)

We'd rather believe the reason is that Hartford was the setting of what is thought to have been the earliest torchlight parade. The organizers were area Republicans called the Hartford Wide-Awakes, and they first marched in 1860 when candidate Abraham Lincoln visited the city. Lincoln won, and the rest is history.

For More Information

Location: The Museum of American Political Life is in the Harry Jack Grey Center on the campus of the University of Hartford, located at 200 Bloomfield Avenue (Route 187) in West Hartford, near the Bloomfield line.

Admission: No charge; donation requested.

Hours: Tuesday through Friday, and Saturday afternoon, year-round, as well as Sunday during the school year.

Contact: Museum of American Political Life, University of Hartford, 200 Bloomfield Avenue, West Hartford, CT 06117; (860) 768-4090.

When in the area: The art-filled Hill-Stead Museum and the colonial Stanley-Whitman House are in the neighboring town of Farmington (Chapter 13).

Lodging: West Hartford Inn, 900 Farmington Avenue, West Hartford, CT; (860) 236-3221. Ramada Inn–Capitol Hill, 440 Asylum Street, Hartford, CT; (860) 246-6591. Goodwin Hotel, 1 Haynes Street (across from the Civic Center), Hartford, CT; (800) 922-5006 or (860) 246-7500. The 1895 House B and B, 97 Girard Avenue, Hartford, CT; (860) 232-0014.

Museum of American Political Life

32

Blackstone River Valley National Heritage Corridor

THIS IS A NATIONAL PARK, BUT IT IS NOT YOUR TYPICAL national park. It is experimental and new, and you don't visit it the way you would visit Yellowstone or Gettysburg. You don't stop at a visitor center and then conveniently walk to a monument or drive a loop road through a preserved site of natural or historical significance.

This is not to say the corridor is not historically significant. The Blackstone River Valley was the birthplace of the American industrial revolution, and the nation's oldest mill complex sits right in the center of Pawtucket, Rhode Island. The national heritage corridor comprises nine towns lining the banks of the Blackstone River in northeastern Rhode Island, from Providence into Woonsocket; it extends up to Worcester, Massachusetts, and runs through parts of an additional twelve towns and cities in the Bay State. (For this book, we are emphasizing only the Rhode Island section of the corridor.)

The National Park Service owns none of the land in the corridor. It oversees the corridor in cooperation with the states of Rhode Island and Massachusetts and various communities and historical associations. Blackstone River Valley National Heritage Corridor is a neat way of tying the towns and sites together. Yet, the sights here, with some exceptions, are not dormant battlefields or unoccupied presidents' homes. Much of the history preserved here includes still active communities whose lifelines were once centered around whirring, droning mills. Park Ranger Peter Coffin says the reason behind forming the national heritage corridor is "to celebrate and preserve a resource that's still living."

What is being celebrated is the industrial revolution and the milling industry, which sprang up along this corridor in the early 1800s, precisely because of the presence of the Blackstone River. The Blackstone has always been the James Brown of waterways, known for generations here as "the hardest working river in America," utilized and employed to the fullest degree. Over the length of its forty-six-mile existence it drops 480 feet, perfect for turning waterwheels and making mill-equipment produce.

Ramble the roads of the towns and villages of the valley and you can easily spot the longtime residents—sturdy, squat, strapping brick structures that once housed rooms of looms and are still topped with long-necked smokestacks, and the cookie-cutter brick houses where folks who worked the mills went home to rest their weary bones.

To those who grew up in villages and towns such as Ashton, Slatersville, and Woonsocket, there is an irony in these places becoming tourist attractions. Says Peter Coffin, "People say, 'What's so special about a mill town? I grew up there, and I couldn't wait to get out.'"

People who spent lifetimes working routine jobs have said that for ages, never realizing they were making history. The list includes trolley operators and steam rail workers, waitresses who carried sandwiches to hungry patrons in downtown diners, and men who chopped chunks of coal from the earth in dusty mines. Today tourists travel miles to ride in authentic trolleys and steam trains, to savor the atmosphere of a classic diner, and to take guided tours of coal mines in Pennsylvania and West Virginia.

Now it's the mill towns' turn.

Fall

The prettiest one in the Blackstone Valley might be Slatersville, with its archetypal New England village green, its stone Arch Bridge, and the four-story Slater Mill, dating from 1826. Homes from the early to mid-1800s where mill owners and workers lived line Green and Main Streets.

Go to Ashton to see the most typical surviving 19th-century mill workers' houses. They are made of brick and sit side by side along Front Street, like the little houses on a Monopoly board. And they are within walking distance of the rambling Ashton Mill, with its rows of windows and practical bell tower. Before mass transit and automobiles, most people lived within walking distance of their places of employment. Today the homes are still lived in, converted into privately owned, federally subsidized apartments.

An alternative to driving to the mills is the *Blackstone Valley Explorer*, a forty-nine-person riverboat that has been sailing the river since 1993. It departs from varied points along the river, and a guide offers a monologue about the human and natural history of the Blackstone.

On our cruise from Woonsocket we sailed past myriad mills, some still churning out products, others converted into housing. We learned that tall mill towers were used as stairways to get from one level to another, and were told about the river's eponym, William Blackstone, who in 1635 became the first European settler in the valley that now bears his name.

A memorial marking the approximate site of Blackstone's grave sits along Broad Street in the village of Lonsdale, part of the town of Cumberland. Appropriately, it is within view of the famous Ann and Hope Mill.

To see the inner workings of an early mill, head to downtown Pawtucket to Slater Mill Historic Site, locally called "the birthplace of American industry." A guided tour lasting from ninety minutes to two hours takes visitors into three buildings huddled along the Blackstone here, all offering

Blackstone River Valley

insight into the evolution of textile making. The Sylvanus Brown House, relocated from elsewhere in town, is restored in a 1758 setting, when spinning and weaving were done by hand.

The second stop is the rubblestone 1810 Wilkinson Mill, a blur of belts and wheels on black machines on which textile-making machinery was produced. Laborers worked six days a week, had no vacations, and could be jailed for laziness if found guilty of not working 100 percent.

Finally, you enter the yellow clapboard Slater Mill, opened in 1793, where fabric was made for nearly eighty years, and filled with early textile-making machinery. Children, whose fingers were conveniently small, were paid thirty-five cents a day to operate throstle spinners, and it was not unusual for a child to lose a little finger or two in fast-turning machine parts.

On beautiful fall days, one can mix a bit of leaf peeping and history by visiting Blackstone Valley State Park, comprising the villages of Albion, Ashton, and Lonsdale in the towns of Cumberland and Lincoln. Stroll along the towpath of the former Blackstone Canal, opened in 1828 to ship goods produced along the river, or canoe the river or a remaining three-mile-long stretch of the canal.

Still, you can't go far without encountering history here. The Kelly House, named for mill owner Wilbur Kelly, borders the canal and is being restored.

FOR MORE INFORMATION

Location: The Rhode Island section of Blackstone River Valley National Heritage Corridor comprises part or all of the towns of Burrillville, Central Falls, Cumberland, Glocester, Lincoln, North Smithfield, Pawtucket, Smithfield, and Woonsocket, and many of the villages nearby.

Admission: A fee is charged for rides on the *Blackstone Valley Explorer* and for Slater Mill Historic Site.

Hours: Rides are offered on the *Explorer* from late April through late October. Slater Mill Historic Site is open March through mid-December, Tuesday through Saturday, and Sunday afternoon.

Contact: Blackstone River Valley National Heritage Corridor, 1 Depot Square, Woonsocket, RI 02895; (401) 762-0250. Slater Mill Historic Site, Roosevelt Avenue, Pawtucket, RI 02860; (401) 725-8638. Blackstone Valley Tourism Council, 171 Main Street, Pawtucket, RI 02860; (800) 454-2882 or (401) 724-2200 (for general information and the *Blackstone Valley Explorer* schedule).

Note: The national heritage corridor is evolving. Plans are in the works for a visitor center museum in Pawtucket, and a bike path to run the length of the corridor, connecting Pawtucket, and Worcester, Massachusetts.

When in the area: Neighboring Providence has extensive colonial history (Chapter 42).

Lodging: Comfort Inn–Providence/Pawtucket, 2 George Street, Pawtucket, RI; (401) 723-6700. Days Hotel on the Harbor, 220 India Street, Providence, RI; (401) 272-5577. Woonsocket Motor Inn, 333 Clinton Street, Woonsocket, RI; (401) 762-1224. Susse Chalet Inn, 355 George Washington Highway, North Smithfield, RI; (401) 232-2400.

33

The Wonders of Hot Air

So, you are seeking a different way to view the fall colors?

And you mean a *different* way.

Consider the wonders of hot air. And we are not referring to a visit to the state legislatures in Hartford and Providence.

We are talking about the magic of floating motionless in the sky, looking down upon the trees, rivers, and whitewashed barns. Welcome to hot-air ballooning.

According to Bruce Byberg, owner of Brighter Skies Ballooning in Woodstock, Connecticut, autumn—for obvious reasons—is the most popular time to take to the skies. A fall flight on a Brighter Skies balloon can take you as high as 3,000 or 4,000 feet above sea level, or so low that you can almost pick a bright red leaf off the top of a towering maple.

Byberg's flights last about an hour, depending on the winds and the terrain, and come with either a morning breakfast or the obligatory glass of champagne, a ballooning tradition that, legend has it, began in Europe when a French balloonist landed in Germany and toasted his host with a bottle of French bubbly. The real high here, though, is not from your basic artificial stimulant, but, as the saying goes, from being at one with nature.

It is the serenity as much as the scenery that Bruce Byberg highlights as a main thrill of a journey by balloon. There is no sensation of movement, Byberg notes. "If you closed your eyes, you'd never know you've left the ground."

It's surprising that the feeling of floating is greater when one is lower to the ground. The reason is that the lower one is, the greater the depth perception. The higher you go, the flatter the landscape looks. Byberg says that when adventure seekers call and say they are considering either a balloon ride or skydiving, he tells them if they're looking for an adrenaline rush, forget the balloon ride. The key word here is *peacefulness*.

A few things to keep in mind when preparing for your sail into the sky: Rides are not cheap; expect to spend between $150 and $225 for about an hour in the sky. Balloons usually take off at sunrise or a few hours before sunset, when winds are calmest and conditions are most stable. Wear loose, comfortable clothing, and sturdy, waterproof boots, since the ground in the early morning can be drenched with dew. Anxious feelings for first-timers are common, says Byberg, but usually dissipate within the first five to ten minutes.

"I took my mother up in a balloon after two years of asking her," Byberg explains. "She was scared at first. Then after ten minutes she was leaning out over the basket and taking pictures."

Despite popular opinion, Byberg says that in his opinion winter is the best time for ballooning. Balloons fly longer and farther in colder weather because the air is denser. He adds that there is nothing like the feeling of flying in a balloon above a fresh, fallen snow.

There are several enterprises offering balloon rides in Connecticut and Rhode Island.

For More Information

Brighter Skies Balloons, 33 Butts Road, Woodstock, CT 06281; (800) 677-5114 or (860) 677-5114.

Fall

Sky Endeavors, 4 Brown Street, Bloomfield, CT 06002; (860) 242-0228.

Airvertising & Airventures, 15 Hedgehog Lane, West Simsbury, CT 06092; (800) 535-2473 or (860) 651-4441.

Kat Balloons, 40 Meadow Lane, Farmington, CT 06032; (860) 678-7921.

Watershed Balloons, 179 Gilbert Road, Watertown, CT 06795; (860) 274-2010.

Steppin' Up Balloons, 258 Old Woodbury Road, Southbury, CT 06488; (203) 264-0013.

Gone Ballooning, 5 Larkey Road, Oxford, CT 06478; (203) 888-1322.

Balloon Hollow Inc., Cold Spring Road, Newtown, CT 06470; (203) 426-4250.

Connecticut Yankee Balloons, 120 Flax Road, Fairfield, CT 06430; (203) 255-1929.

Stumpf Balloons, PO Box 913, Bristol, RI 02809; (401) 253-0111.

The Wonders of Hot Air

34

Come to the Fairs

THE ROAR, THE GREASE, THE SMELLS, THE CROWDS. THIS chapter is not about theater, although some might consider the traditional agricultural fair a true American showpiece. Broadway legends Rodgers and Hammerstein even crafted a musical called *State Fair*, now considered a classic. But the event itself might be the most basic form of all-American entertainment.

There are the cattle on parade, the home-baked apple pies, the tractor-pulling contests, the midway, the fried dough, the quilts, the crafts, the canning, the horse-pulling contests, the barbecues, the country music, the hot dogs, the hogs, the ponies.

Neither Connecticut nor Rhode Island has a state fair, but each boasts dozens of other major fairs, along with district fairs, 4-H fairs, and local fairs. The biggest of all is the Durham Fair, held annually in late September, in Durham, Connecticut.

In an average year with good weather, the three-day event garners a quarter of a million people. It measures a half mile from one end of the Durham fairgrounds to the other. There are animals galore and major names in the world of music.

The animals, of course, are the raison d'être of Durham and other fairs. Surveys have shown the animals to be the top draw for visitors. But if you are at a total loss as to the mechanics of animal judging, you are in good company. According to Durham Fair president Leonard Baginski, persons actively involved in farming are the exception among visitors. Most who come to the fair are as familiar with what constitutes an award-winning dairy cow as Woody Allen.

Basically, animals are judged by their potential value as products. Beef cattle and pigs are judged by their muscle tone. In dairy cattle, udders are the utter consideration. In sheep, it's both muscle tone and the quality of their wool. Other competitions, such as horse pulling and ox pulling, are judged by sheer numbers, such as time and weight.

Many animal fanciers could not care less about judging. They want to pet and touch the animals, or perhaps admire handsome home-grown produce and handmade crafts. "It's a way to get back to grandmother's day, or actually great-grandmother's day," remarks Baginski.

Surveys, Baginski adds, show that after animals, visitors most like entertainment. Country or country rock stars are most likely to take the stage. Durham performers in recent years have included Holly Dunn, Steve Warner, John Hartford, the Nitty Gritty Dirt Band, and the Marshall Tucker Band. Golden oldies performers, such as Jan & Dean, have been known to step up to the microphone, too.

Baginski says that the midway is ranked low among visitor favorites. At the Durham Fair the midway is set off by itself away from the other fair components. Those turned off by the midway, Baginski notes, can simply avoid it.

Midway games have gotten a bad rap in recent years from consumer and investigative reporters who have shown games at some carnivals to be fixed and impossible to win. Baginski stresses that Connecticut has strict standards. Games are inspected by the State Police, and midway rides are inspected by the State Fire Marshall's Office. "We haven't had to close anything down since I don't know when," he says.

The history of the Durham Fair is long. The first was held October 4, 1916, and was a purely agricultural exhibition. There was a parade down Main Street, along with oxen and horses and fruit-and-vegetable displays. Admission was twenty-five cents for adults and ten cents for children.

A contemporary local newspaper, the *Penny Press*, wrote of the debut fair, "Without a single question the Durham Fair was a success. It brought the community together in a common interest, stimulated friendly rivalry in exhibition and production . . . We do not hesitate to predict that if Durham sees fit to repeat this venture another year there will be a larger response and a larger success."

Though we may take them for granted, amusements were not allowed until 1926. The Coleman Brothers were permitted to set up a carousel that year, but a Ferris wheel was specifically prohibited.

Only acts of God and madmen have halted the fair. The famous 1938 hurricane was cause for canceling the fair that year. It was also canceled from 1942 to 1944.

If you cannot make it to Durham, consider other quality fairs. Our sources tell us that Connecticut's best are at Durham, Hebron, and Woodstock, the latter two taking place in early September. (Although we have slotted agricultural fairs in the fall section of this book, some occur as early as mid-summer, others as late as mid-October.)

Other top fairs are in Bethlehem (early September), Brooklyn (late August), Goshen (early September), Guilford (late September), Haddam Neck (early September), and Harwinton (early October).

Rhode Islanders have slim pickings. The state has just one agricultural extravaganza, the Washington

Come to the Fairs

County Fair, taking place in mid-August at the fairgrounds in Richmond.

For More Information

Contact: Bethlehem Fair, (203) 266-5350; Brooklyn Fair, (860) 779-0012; Durham Fair, (860) 349-9495; Goshen Fair, (860) 491-3085; Guilford Fair, (203) 453-3543; Haddam Neck Fair, (860) 267-0628; Harwinton Fair, (860) 485-1821; Hebron Fair, (860) 228-0892; Washington County Fair, (401) 783-2070; Woodstock Fair, (860) 928-5711.

For a directory of Connecticut's agricultural fairs, including dates and specific activities, contact: The Association of Connecticut Fairs, PO Box 753, Somers, CT 06071. A self-addressed stamped envelope with $1.00 return postage is requested.

Lodging: Dan'l Merwin House B and B (built in 1740), 308 Main Street, Durham, CT; (860) 349-8415. Ramada Inn, 275 Research Parkway, Meriden, CT; (203) 238-2380. Hampton Inn, 10 Bee Street, Meriden, CT; (203) 235-5154. Middletown Motor Inn, 988 Washington Street, Middletown, CT; (860) 346-9251. The Rowson House (B and B in a circa-1920 Colonial Revival home), 53 Prospect Street, Middletown, CT; (860) 346-8479.

35

For the Birds

MILAN BULL, DIRECTOR OF THE CONNECTICUT AUDUBON Society in Fairfield, has two suggestions for novices interested in taking up bird-watching:

"Learn how to look. Learn how to see."

And what does that mean?

"To look is to look for movement in the trees. To see is to interpret the movement," Bull explains. "Is the bird bobbing up and down? Is it twitching its tail?"

After that, says Bull, try to get a look at the size and shape of the bird's beak to help identify it. Then notice its habitat: whether it's perched atop a tree, sitting in a bush, or resting on a pond. With a little practice and experience, you can start identifying birds' physical features, such as their coloring and calls.

Any season is a good season to look for the birds, but in fall you have the double advantage of bright foliage joining radiant plumage. Early fall is also migratory season, a good time to see songbirds and hawks.

Longtime birders say being at one with nature is a major attraction of their favorite pastime. "It gives you an appreciation of your environment," explains Hap Morgan, education coordinator of the Norman Bird Sanctuary and Museum in Middletown, Rhode Island. "I like being outdoors and experiencing the different elements and habitats."

Like Milan Bull, Morgan advises beginners to listen for movement first, then watch. Bull and Morgan have other suggestions for first-timers:

1. Approach the area quietly.

2. Go early in the morning. About 6:30 A.M. or earlier is best. As the day warms up, birds take refuge in the underbrush and become quieter. Late sleepers might try evenings. In fall, 5:30 P.M. or later is recommended.

3. Take a field guide with you. Noticing a bird's idiosyncrasies won't do any good unless you can identify it. Both Morgan and Bull say *Peterson's Field Guide to Birds of the East* is the Bible among bird-watchers. (Author Roger Tory Peterson died in July 1996 at his home in Old Lyme, Connecticut, at the age of eighty-seven.)

   Other suggested field guides are *National Geographic Guide to North American Birds*, *Golden Guide to Birds of North America*, and *Stokes Field Guide to Birds* (Eastern edition).

4. Take binoculars.

5. Dress for the weather and wear comfortable shoes.

6. Go with a group, and feel free to ask other bird-watchers what they have seen that day.

7. Frustration is natural. As with any avocation, you will have both good and bad days. Don't let one day of frustration turn you off to bird-watching.

8. Head to the beach. Shorebirds are among the most exciting to see in motion.

Both men recommend Lighthouse Point, a city park in New Haven, as a prime place to see raptors. Phone (203) 946-8005. Bull says it has the largest concentration of raptors in the state. "They have counted as many as 30,000 hawks in one day in September and October," he reports.

Bull also endorses the Connecticut Audubon Center at Milford Point in Milford. Phone (203) 878-7440. It has boardwalks, observation platforms and towers, and interpretive signage. According to Bull, it is one of the best areas between Maine and New York for spotting migrating shorebirds, raptors, waterfowl, and endangered species such as least terns and piping plovers.

Another of Bull's suggestions is Hammonasset Beach State Park in Madison, for owls, shorebirds, and waterfowl. Phone (203) 245-2785. There is also the roughly 160-acre Roy and Margot Larsen Sanctuary at the Connecticut Audubon Society in Fairfield, Bull's own base. It has a birds-of-prey compound.

Away from the shore? Bull favors White Memorial Foundation in Litchfield to see a diverse number of inland songbirds and rails. Phone (860) 567-0857. Another inland location, though perhaps a better summer than fall birdwatching locale, is Connecticut Audubon at Trail Wood in Hampton, where nesting birds put on a show. Phone (860) 455-0759.

In Rhode Island, Hap Morgan suggests a stop at his Norman Bird Sanctuary in Middletown. The sanctuary's Hanging Rock Trail affords a vantage point for hawk migration, which hits its peak in mid-October, and its Second and Third beaches are stopovers for migrating songbirds. Red-tailed hawks peak here in late October, and ospreys, Cooper's hawks, broad-winged hawks, and marsh hawks can be seen, too.

The sanctuary's ponds are refuges for waterfowl from October into December. American widgeons, black ducks, and gadwalls are frequently seen in Gray Craig Pond. On larger Gardiner's Pond keep your eyes out for diving ducks called scaups and ruddy ducks. Canada geese can be seen here by late fall.

Morgan also likes Great Swamp Management Area in South Kingstown, (401) 789-0281, and various preserves

For the Birds

scattered along the south coast. Included are Sachuest Point National Wildlife Refuge in Middletown, (401) 364-9124, just outside the Norman Bird Sanctuary; Galilee Bird Sanctuary, (401) 789-3094, and Trustom Pond National Wildlife Refuge, (401) 364-9124 or (401) 421-5055, in South Kingstown; and Ninigret National Wildlife Refuge, (401) 364-1222, and Kimball Wildlife Refuge, (401) 364-3074, in Charlestown.

FOR MORE INFORMATION

Contact: Norman Bird Sanctuary, (401) 846-2577; Connecticut Audubon Center at Fairfield, (203) 259-6305.

For recorded information of latest bird sightings: In Rhode Island, the Voice of Audubon, (401) 949-3870; in Connecticut, Bird Alert, (203) 254-3665.

36

Exploring the Brass City

I GREW UP IN SUBURBAN HARTFORD, YET THE ONLY THING I knew about Waterbury was that it was the place you drove through to get to New York City. Like many other people, my attitude about Waterbury had been "There's nothing to do there," mainly because I had never been there.

What I have since learned is that Waterbury is an ethnically rich city with a sizable share of classic homes, a spacious green, and a lot of hidden history. The best place to begin an exploration is Waterbury's cultural headquarters, the Mattatuck Museum.

At the Mattatuck you get to see how the other half lived, regardless of which half you were part of. The history of the Naugatuck Valley is presented on the first floor by way of a walk-through re-created factory, living rooms and parlors that would have been found in area homes throughout the centuries, and even the counter of a turn-of-the-century Waterbury saloon. Probate inventories were used to re-create the home interiors as accurately as possible.

Representing the 17th-century farm village of colonial Waterbury is the interior of the home of a man named Daniel Warner, with its obligatory spinning wheel and rope bed. Farther along in the museum is the plush Victorian sitting room of entrepreneur James Scovill. Directly across from Scovill's digs is the Spartan kitchen of Edmund Fitzpatrick, immigrant from Ireland and one of Scovill's factory workers.

Later on you reach the early 1900s with Sven Olsen's saloon, known as "the poor man's club," and a typical Waterbury triple-decker with laundry hanging on a clothesline high above.

The Mattatuck also tips its hat to Waterbury's industry, especially the gazillions of brass buttons once made here. Pass through a re-created brass button factory, built narrow with large windows for a reason: such a factory would have been illuminated only by daylight which would have been unable to illuminate a wide room.

Waterbury's contributions to industry went beyond brass. Pocket watches made here became known across the nation as "Waterbury watches." Aluminum was first fabricated here, and the Mickey Mouse watch was patented here in 1933; the original rodent wristwatch patent is posted. And no one who visits the Mattatuck forgets Charles Goodyear's rubber desk, a Goodyear invention that never quite took off the way his tires did.

Upstairs is a gallery paying tribute to artists with a Connecticut connection. You will see works by famous Americans such as John Trumbull, Alexander Calder, J. Alden and John Ferguson Weir, and Frederick Church. Church might be best known as a member of the Hudson River school of painting, but he was the son of an insurance executive, born and raised in Hartford. He decided to forgo his father's field and made the art world the beneficiary of his talents. Examine Church's *Icebergs*, painted off the coast of Labrador, and be dazzled by colors reflecting off the ice.

Then step outside the Mattatuck and take in the real-life landscape of Waterbury's spacious city green. The houses of the city's first settlers surrounded the green, which was used for grazing. The contemporary Veterans Memorial adds a modern touch to the historic two-acre patch of verdancy.

For a later historic locale, step behind the Mattatuck and take a walk or drive through Hillside, one of Waterbury's revived neighborhoods and the one where the Scovills and other area brass magnates lived. A brochure available at the Mattatuck outlines a tour.

When we visited, we saw Victorian homes in the Queen Anne and Italianate villa styles alongside Gothic and Greek Revival houses. Some needed a good fixing up, while others looked as if the hammer had just hit the final nail. Don't miss the Benedict-Miller House, an elaborate Victorian jewel at 32 Hillside Avenue and part of the campus of the Waterbury branch of the University of Connecticut. Rose Hill, at 63 Prospect Street, is an 1852 house with a heavy Gothic-style influence. The neighborhood is fairly safe, but you may want to skip an after-dark walking tour if you're by yourself.

For some more noteworthy architecture, take Leaven-worth Street from the green to Grand Street. Near the corner of Grand and Leavenworth is the Cass Gilbert Historic District. Several buildings in this area, including the sprawling City Hall and Chase Municipal Building, were designed by Gilbert, one of 19th-century America's leading architects. Overlooking the whole city is the clock tower at 389 Meadow, based on the tower in the center of Siena, Italy.

FOR MORE INFORMATION

Location: The Mattatuck Museum is at 144 West Main Street, facing the green.

Admission: No charge.

Hours: The Mattatuck Museum is open Tuesday through Saturday, and Sunday afternoon, from September through June; it is closed Sunday in summer.

Contact: Mattatuck Museum, 144 West Main Street, Waterbury, CT 06702; (203) 753-0381. Waterbury Region Convention & Visitors Bureau (for information on historic neigh-borhoods), PO Box 1469, Waterbury, CT 06721; (203) 579-9527.

When in the area: Consider exploring another chunk of urban culture at New Haven's Yale University (Chapter 46).

Lodging: Quality Inn, 88 Union Street, Waterbury, CT; (203) 575-1500. Courtyard by Marriott, 63 Grand Street, Waterbury, CT; (203) 596-1000. Seventy Hillside (a mansion built in 1901, now a B and B), 70 Hillside Avenue, Waterbury, CT; (203) 596-7070. House on the Hill (a Victorian-era B and B), 92 Woodlawn Terrace, Waterbury, CT; (203) 757-9901.

Fall

37

Colonial Newport

MENTION HISTORY IN NEWPORT, RHODE ISLAND, AND THE immediate association is the Gilded Age—mansions, millionaires, and the social elite—for only those with the right bearings, breeding, and background could become part of Newport's high society. No matter how much wealth one had attained, those who practiced the "wrong" religion didn't fit in.

There is a little touch of irony, however, in this leisure-minded seaport town, since the deepest roots of religious liberty in the United States are planted just a few miles from the exclusive summer palaces lining Bellevue Avenue. At 85 Touro Street is the oldest Jewish house of worship in the United States, the Touro Synagogue, a living remnant of Newport's storied colonial history and a testament to the colony's religious liberty.

But as important as Touro Synagogue National Historic Site is for its embodiment of religious freedom, it is also an architectural gem, designed by one of colonial America's most respected architects, Peter Harrison. Harrison adapted the synagogue to the styles of his time by applying the principles of Georgian architecture: symmetry, balance, and ordered rhythm. But he modified it somewhat to conform to Sephardic Jewish ritual; it was planned so that the building would sit in a diagonal position in order for the congregation to face eastward toward Jerusalem when standing before the Ark (the chest containing the Torah used in services).

The guided tour of the interior emphasizes the original furnishings. A deerskin Torah (Scroll of the Law) resting in a protective glass-enclosed case is authentic. So is a painting of the Ten Commandments sitting above the Ark.

Within walking distance of Touro Synagogue is Newport's oldest residence, the Wanton-Lyman-Hazard House. The date of construction has been verified to be somewhere between 1675 and 1690. Newport Historical Society historian Pieter Roos notes that while other Newport buildings may contain older remnants, no older house is standing in its entirety.

All the furniture in the Wanton-Lyman-Hazard House is authentic to the period. The original floorboards are easily recognizable for their exposed knots. The biggest curiosity might be the grandmother's chair, also known as an invalid's chair. It would have been used by an elderly person or an infirm child and was easily moved from one room and one floor to another.

In 1993 the Newport Historical Society opened the Museum of Newport History, where laser-disc technology combines with antique artifacts to tell the story of this city, from Native Americans who settled here 12,000 years ago through the Gilded Age. Colonial times are afforded emphasis with 18th-century silver, oil portraits, and furniture made by Townsend and Goddard, Newport's premier 18th- and 19th-century furniture makers.

The Newport Historical Society also offers guided walking tours of both the colonial historic area and the Cliff Walk.

About a half century after the Wanton-Lyman-Hazard House took form, a politician and ship owner named Jonathan Nichols Jr. constructed a house, a wharf, and warehouses on Water Street, later to be renamed Washington Street.

After the Revolutionary War ended, Newport's busy port closed, and the city suffered economic tough times. The

Fall

house that Nichols built, along with many other Newport homes, fell into disrepair. In 1805 an attorney named William Hunter bought the Nichols house for $5,000 and made it his family's residence for more than fifty years.

Known today as the Hunter House, it breathes quiet formality and is best known among design historians for its accurately restored interior. Note the carved paneling in the northeast parlor with its faux (false) marble, black and gold pilasters, and baseboards. Townsend and Goddard furniture is in abundance.

FOR MORE INFORMATION

Location: Touro Synagogue is at 85 Touro Street in midtown Newport.

Admission: No charge.

Hours: July and August, daily, except Saturday (open Saturday for religious services only); late spring and early to mid-fall, Sunday and weekday early afternoons; rest of the year, Sunday early afternoons and weekday afternoons by appointment only.

Contact: Touro Synagogue National Historic Site, 85 Touro Street, Newport, RI 02840; (401) 847-4794.

Location: Wanton-Lyman-Hazard House is at 17 Broadway in midtown Newport. Museum of Newport History is at the Brick Market on Thames Street at the foot of Washington Square.

Admission: A fee is charged for both the house and museum and for walking tours.

Hours: Wanton-Lyman-Hazard House is open June and September, Friday through Sunday; July and August, Thursday through Saturday, and Sunday afternoon; or by appointment. Museum of Newport History is open April through December, Monday, Wednesday through Saturday, and Sunday afternoon. Walking tours are offered Thursday through Saturday. A self-guided walking tour of the historic district is also available.

Contact: Newport Historical Society, 82 Touro Street, Newport, RI 02840; (401) 846-0813. Museum of Newport History, (401) 841-8770.

Location: Hunter House is at 54 Washington Street in the section of Newport known as the Point, north of midtown.

Admission: A fee is charged.

Hours: May through September, daily; October and April, weekends.

Contact: Preservation Society of Newport County, 424 Bellevue Avenue, Newport, RI 02840; (401) 847-1000.

When in the area: Also open through much or all of the fall are Newport's many mansions (Chapter 3), the International Tennis Hall of Fame (Chapter 19), and the Museum of Yachting and the Naval War College Museum (Chapter 15).

Lodging: This is the B and B capital of southern New England. A partial list of Newport B and Bs includes: Cliffside Inn (former home of artist Beatrice Turner and repository for many of her works), 2 Seaview Avenue; (800) 845-1811 or (401) 847-1811. The Wayside, 406 Bellevue Avenue; (401) 847-0302. The Jailhouse Inn (a restored colonial jail), 13 Marlborough Street; (401) 847-4638. Brinley Victorian Inn, 23 Brinley Street; (800) 999-8523 or (401) 849-7645. The Willows, 8-10 Willow Street; (401) 846-5486.

There is also a B and B service listing rooms in more than 150 private homes, inns, and guest houses: Anna's Victorian Connection, 5 Fowler Avenue, Newport, RI 02840; (800) 884-4288 or (401) 849-2489.

Conventional motels in Newport include: Motel 6, 249 J. T. Connell Highway; (401) 848-0600. Best Western Mainstay Inn, 151 Admiral Kalbfus Road; (401) 849-9880. Newport Harbor Hotel & Marina, 49 America's Cup Avenue; (401) 847-9000.

38

Fort Griswold State Park

THE BATTLE OF GROTON HEIGHTS GARNERS LESS THAN A paragraph in many tomes devoted to the American Revolution. In some volumes, it doesn't account for a footnote.

But in southern New England, it ranks as one of the most notorious events in the region's history. Like Bennington in Vermont and Bunker Hill in Boston, its place in history is marked with a monument and a museum. But unlike Bennington and Bunker Hill, this one marks the site of not a victory or a show of strength, but a massacre.

Bloody past aside, the spectacular view from this patch of local history makes for an inviting early-fall visit.

But why is this relatively minor battle of major interest here?

First, Groton Heights was the only battle of any significance fought on Connecticut soil. Second, it has been ranked as one of the most brutal massacres in the Revolution. Third, it provided the last moment of glory for Brigadier General Benedict Arnold, a native Connecticut Yankee who would sail to England three months later, never to return.

As you climb the bluffs here and take in the panorama of the Thames and neighboring New London, you realize why this was an ideal setting for a fortification. On September 6, 1781, Fort Griswold, on the east bank of the river, was in good shape, with a full magazine. Not so for the west bank where Fort Trumbull was still incomplete and vulnerable, even as late as September 1781.

Arnold landed his fleet on both sides of the Thames on the night of September 5. The next morning, his troops easily seized Fort Trumbull and set fires to ships, wharves, and public buildings. A warehouse with a supply of gunpowder exploded, spreading fiery debris throughout New London. Residents ran with children in their arms to safety.

Fort Griswold, on the east side of the Thames, proved more stubborn. Connecticut commander Lieutenant Colonel William Ledyard was expecting reinforcements when the British called for surrender. Ledyard refused. In the ensuing British advance, Ledyard was killed. American accounts say that when Ledyard offered his sword, British Major Stephen Bromfield pushed it through Ledyard's heart.

But despite the carnage in Connecticut, the battle did not change the course of events. George Washington was on his way south and soon trapped General Cornwallis at Yorktown, Virginia, ending the war.

Looking at the busy waterfront today, it is difficult to imagine the muskets and mayhem of more than two hundred years ago. But as you wander through the fort's remains, historic markers remind you of the massacre and one indicates the exact spot where "Colonel Ledyard fell by his own sword in the hand of the British officer to whom he had surrendered in the massacre of Fort Griswold, September 6, 1781."

The sword is the main attraction in the small museum. Firearms, uniforms, and a cannon keep it company, while engravings of Benedict Arnold help illustrate the story. A model of Fort Griswold as it appeared the morning of the battle will help you visualize the setting.

You can reach the top of the monument by climbing 166 calf-wrenching steps of a spiral staircase. On the proverbial clear day, your view extends to Long Island. Or you can spy into the activities of the nearby submarine base.

Fall

For More Information

Location: To get to Fort Griswold State Park, take exit 87 from Interstate 95. The fort is one and a half miles south of Route 1 at the corner of Monument Street and Park Avenue.

Admission: No charge.

Hours: Daily, Memorial Day through Labor Day, and weekends after Labor Day through Columbus Day. In summer, one can visit the Avery House, a ten-room colonial home and also part of the park.

Contact: Fort Griswold Battlefield State Park, 57 Fort Street, Groton, CT 06340; (203) 445-1729 for general park information or (203) 449-6877 for the museum.

When in the area: A look at submarine life, legend, and lore is yours at the USS *Nautilus* Memorial and its adjacent museum, while an inspection of the rigors of life at a military academy awaits across the Thames at the U.S. Coast Guard Academy (Chapter 2).

Lodging: Quality Inn, 404 Bridge Street, Groton, CT; (860) 445-8141. Groton Inn & Suites, 99 Gold Star Highway (Route 184), Groton, CT; (800) 452-2191 or (860) 445-9784. Red Roof Inn, 707 Colman Street, New London, CT; (860) 444-0001. Queen Anne Inn (a Victorian inn with antique furnishings), 265 Williams Street, New London, CT; (800) 347-8818 or (860) 447-2600.

Fort Griswold State Park

39

Halloween

WHY IS IT THAT WE ARE BOTH REPULSED AND FASCINATED BY the grisly? We are disgusted by auto accidents, but we slow down as we drive past. We are sickened by the lurid truths about Ted Bundy or Jeffrey Dahmer, but we read the news reports just the same.

On Halloween, we are permitted socially to show our dark sides. This is the holiday made for the stuff that gives us the creeps, and there are plenty of places in southern New England to get them.

The Witch's Dungeon

The brainchild of Bristol, Connecticut artist Cortlandt Hull, this seasonal dungeon has become one of New England's premier Halloween events. As you step inside, the voice of actor Vincent Price chortles, "Welcome, poor mortal, to this witch's dungeon of nightmares." Price recorded the monologue before his death in 1993. (In most cases, that statement might seem obvious. But Halloween isn't "most cases.")

Inside Hull's own seasonal horror museum, you wander through narrow corridors where you meet life-size replicas of classic movie monsters such as Count Dracula, the Phantom of the Opera, and the Wolfman, who speak thanks to custom-made tapes and edited movie soundtracks. The voice of Zenobia, the Gypsy Witch, is actress June Foray, who did witch voices in classic Bugs Bunny cartoons (although she is best known as the voice of Rocky the Flying Squirrel).

Says Zenobia as you approach her, "Come closer to the cauldron, Dearie. Old Zenobia is brewing a delectable concoction just for you, with a pinch of mummy powder, some shrunken hearts, a sprinkling of lizard gizzards, and, oh yes, a cup of eyeballs to improve your vision."

Admission is nominal, and the Witch's Dungeon is hardly a moneymaker. Then, why does Hull do it? "For the love of the actors and makeup artists that created the classic films and to remind a new generation of them," he answers.

The Witch's Dungeon is open the last two weekends in October, Friday through Sunday evenings. People come from surrounding states to walk through Hull's creation, so expect a wait—an hour or more is not uncommon. And if you have kids under age six, leave them at home.

Contact: (860) 583-8306.

Trolley Terror

Rails to the Dark Side is the name of the thirty-minute-long trolley jaunt offered at the Connecticut Trolley Museum in East Windsor. Legend has it that trolley tracks were built over an ancient graveyard, so it's not surprising that the spirits of the dead come back every Halloween season to exact revenge on those who disturbed their final resting places. You might meet a band of ghouls holding severed heads, or avenging ghosts ready to conduct human sacrifices. It's best to keep the youngsters home for this one.

As an alternative for little ones, the museum hosts Halloween parties the last two weekends in October. More benign activities such as face painting, scavenger hunts, beanbag tosses, and goodie bags with toys and yummy stuff to eat are on tap.

Admission: A fee is charged.

Contact: Connecticut Trolley Museum, (860) 627-6540.

The Shoreline Trolley Museum in East Haven has for years hosted Trolley Tricks 'n' Treats but is considering closing the event for liability reasons. To check on the latest developments, call the museum: (203) 467-6927.

Edgar Allen Poe Day

On one special day at the Astors' Beechwood in Newport, Rhode Island, actors perform skits from Poe's works. The program varies from year to year, but expect to see interpretations of "The Pit and the Pendulum," "The Fall of the House of Usher," or "The Raven." (So far, no critic has said, "Nevermore.")

Also lasting through Halloween are the Astors' Murder Mystery tours. As is usual for special events here, a mansion tour of Beechwood is included. The murder mystery is child friendly, although the Poe performances are recommended for those ages eight or older.

Admission: A fee is charged.

Contact: (401) 846-3772.

Spooky Zoo Halloween

Meet the creepy crawlies head-on. You can come face to face with snakes, bats, toads, spiders, and tarantulas that reside at Roger Williams Park Zoo in Providence at this one-day event. There is a haunted house, a costume parade, face and pumpkin painting, and an event called Spine-Tingling Story Telling. The scariest thing for some kids is that they might actually learn something at this fun event; scavenger hunt participants search the zoo to answer questions about resident animals.

Admission: A fee is charged. Children age twelve and under in costume enter free.

Contact: (401) 785-3510.

Ghosts Along the Blackstone

You never know what you will encounter while riding the riverboat *Blackstone Valley Explorer* on a Haunted Boat Ride along the Blackstone River in Woonsocket, Rhode Island. Folks dressed as dinosaurs or fifteen-foot-tall man-eating trees might jump from the banks onto the boat. Or you just might be invaded by a band of pirates. Special effects, such as strobes, explosions, and fake fog, are constants. About six rides are offered nightly for roughly the two weeks before Halloween, and trips last about twenty minutes.

Recently, Haunted Trolley Tours, aboard a replica of an old trolley, have taken place during Halloween season on the old Blackstone Canal bed in Woonsocket. Expect to meet unannounced guests here, too, such as the ghost of an old canal boat captain.

Both boat and trolley rides are fine for kids of grade-school age and older.

Admission: A fee is charged.

Contact: (401) 724-1500 (the *Explorer's* direct number); (800) 454-2882 or (401) 724-2200 for the Blackstone Valley Tourism Council.

Winter

40

Dashing Through the Snow

THERE ARE WINTER OUTDOOR ACTIVITIES IN NEW ENGLAND for the nonathlete. Even in these days of cyberspace and cable television, when we can spend an entire winter weekend without leaving the house and still be entertained, many of us can't resist those mornings when one just wants to jump headfirst into a Currier and Ives lithograph.

Luckily, there are plenty of places to do something about those fuzzy feelings of nostalgia. Several enterprises in southern New England offer old-fashioned sleigh rides over the river, through the woods, under a starry winter canopy, or along the frosty mantel of a sugary white field.

Some of the following places will arrange a bonfire or snacks upon your return from the ride. Others are more basic. Many supply blankets, but it is a good idea to take your own as an extra. A wool hat, gloves, and boots are essentials in order to keep warm, regardless of whom you snuggle up next to. Jewelry is best kept at home; looking for a ring in heaps of snow is no fun. If you want to take along a wine flask, most places won't care. They just ask that behavior doesn't get out of hand. But it's best to ask in advance.

When snow is sparse, hayrides are usually substituted, and you are transported on wheels rather than runners. Whether that affects the mood of what you had in mind is up to you.

Following is a list of enterprises offering sleigh rides in Connecticut and Rhode Island:

Allegra Farm   Route 82, East Haddam, CT 06483; (860) 873-9658. Kate and John Allegra offer rides on three small antique sleighs that hold from two to nine persons. Rides last from fifteen minutes to an hour and traverse pasture-lands and woods. An outdoor winter campfire is usually raging on weekends, but BYOHDM (bring your own hot dogs and marshmallows) for roasting. You can drop in on a weekend (late mornings or afternoons), or make a reservation.

Chepachet Farms   226 Tourtellot Hill Road, Chepachet, RI 02814; (401) 568-9996. Sleigh rides here last about an hour, and two sleighs are used. A small antique sleigh more than one hundred years old seats three. A newly built bob sleigh seats from ten to twelve. You can pet farm animals in a barn while waiting for your ride and sip hot chocolate by a fire upon your return. Reservations required.

Christmas House   1557 Ten Rod Road, Exeter, RI 02822; (401) 397-4255. Rides are offered here during Christmas season only. Two newly built Austrian-style sleighs are pulled usually by Belgian horses, and each ride lasts twenty to thirty minutes. About thirteen to fifteen persons can be accommodated on each sleigh. Hot chocolate is served, and on weekends the red-suited, bearded guy himself is in attendance. Drop-ins are welcome on weekends, or you can make a reservation.

Flamig Farm   West Mountain Road, West Simsbury, CT 06092; (860) 658-5070. A team of Belgian draft horses pulls you across logging roads and open fields. A total of four sleighs are used; three are antiques. Two sleighs are small, holding two to four riders, while two large ones can handle up to sixteen passengers. Rides last twenty minutes. On some weekends you can follow your ride with hot chocolate and other snacks while recorded music is piped into the barn. During Christmas season, Santa makes appearances. Reservations required.

Jim Thimpson   840 Stony Lane, North Kingstown, RI 02852; (401) 294-6447. Jim has a pung sleigh which can hold up to a half dozen riders. Belgians will pull you for about a half hour through woods and fields. No extras. Reservations required.

John W. Cole   6 Adelaide Road (off Route 44), Chepachet, RI 02814; (401) 568-9303. Cole reports that his Belgians are bilingual. "They take commands in both French and English," he boasts. They also take riders through the woods of northern Rhode Island on a pung (capacity fourteen), or a smaller sleigh (capacity four). No extras. No reservations needed; just show up on a Saturday or Sunday during daylight hours as long as snow covers the ground.

Loon Meadow Farm   Loon Meadow Drive, Norfolk, CT 06058; (860) 542-6085. The owners here maintain four antique sleighs which are pulled by Belgians and Percherons through the northwestern Connecticut woods. Two of the sleighs are best for couples or small families, while the other two seat ten and twelve persons. Hot mulled cider is offered afterwards, and a blazing bonfire can be arranged in advance. A three-room bed-and-breakfast is on the grounds. Reservations required.

Roseland Acres   594 East Road, Tiverton, RI 02878; (401) 624-8866. A Haflinger and perhaps a Morgan will pull your sleigh through the woods and open fields of southeastern Rhode Island. There are two sleighs—a century-old egg-shaped model seating three, and a newly built buckboard sleigh seating six. Rides take thirty to forty-five minutes and,

Dashing Through the Snow

depending on the weather, might be followed by an outdoor campfire where you can roast marshmallows. Hot chocolate is served regardless of the meteorological conditions. Reservations required.

Ross's Farm   22 Paine Road, Foster, RI 02825; (401) 647-7230. There are four sleighs here, all dating to the 19th century and holding from two to five people. Rides last from thirty to forty-five minutes, and don't be surprised if the driver offers you the chance to hold the reins for a while. Warm up afterwards with hot chocolate by a stove indoors. Reservations required.

Wimler Farm   Route 77 (Guilford Road), Durham, CT 06422; (860) 349-3190. Upwards of twenty persons can be carried on each of two big wooden sleds pulled by Belgians. Rides last about an hour and traverse acres of wooded grounds. Reservations required.

Windy Hill Farm   Kick Hill Road, Lebanon, CT 06249; (860) 642-6188. The Scanlon family takes passengers for rides on two antique bobsleds, holding fifteen and from twenty to twenty-five, respectively. American and European Belgians know the way around the open fields of this dairy farm located atop a windy hill (naturally!). Rides last about an hour. Visitors bring their own refreshments and can chow down and relax in a barn. Reservations required.

Wood Acres   Griffin Road, Terryville, CT 06786; (860) 583-8670. Percherons pull either a small sleigh holding four or a large bobsled supporting fourteen on rides lasting just under an hour. Owners Ken and Joyce Wood also own and maintain a horse-drawn trolley. Snacks are served indoors after the ride. The Woods will bring a sleigh ride to you if you wish. "We travel all over New England," says Joyce Wood. Reservations required.

Ye Plain Ole Farm   30 Kerr Road, Canterbury, CT 06331; (860) 546-1079. Two big bobsleds with a capacity of fifteen to twenty persons each are used at this northeastern Connecticut farm. Pulling them are teams of either Belgians or American creams which, according to owner Doug Smith, are the only breed of draft horse that originated in North America. Rides are flexible, depending on the patron's wishes, but usually last about forty-five minutes. Hot cider or coffee and doughnuts are served afterwards. Reservations required.

Dashing Through the Snow

41

Early American Hearth Tours

WHERE DRAINED TRAVELERS ONCE WAITED WEARILY FOR THE next canal boat, you are afforded the chance to help cook and then dine on a sumptuous 1830s-style meal. Where Tories were held prisoner during the American Revolution, you can have tea in honor of George Washington's birthday. Where tasty tea cakes were served during the reign of Queen Victoria, you get to sample the same.

These events are the high points of three Early American Hearth Tours, offered for your indulgence by the Farmington Valley Visitors Association in the comfortable western and northern suburbs of Hartford. Each affords a taste—both literal and figurative—of life here long ago, and each takes place during the long winter when it sometimes seems that skiers are the only people who know how to keep busy.

The old canal tavern called the Phelps House, part of Simsbury's historic Massacoh Plantation, is one setting for "Open Hearth Cooking Along an Old Canal." The canal in question is the Farmington Canal, which flowed from New Haven to Northampton, Massachusetts, from 1829 to 1849, before the railroad made it obsolete. Simsbury was midway along the route, and many transients paused here before continuing their journeys.

It is in this old canal tavern that "Open Hearth Cooking" participants churn butter, chop carrots, and whip cream as they prepare dinner the 1830s way. The preparation time involved shocks most late-20th-century visitors. Cream is whipped by hand with a birch twig. One guest commented, "My family would starve to death before I got this ready."

You do get to savor the finished product, commonly stew or chicken fricassee, winter vegetables, corn bread, fruited rice pudding, or syllabub (a beverage or gelatin dessert made from liquor and sweet milk or cream). And the setting is enviable—by candle and firelight with flames glowing in the two colonial fireplaces.

The Tories were held captive in the Sarah Whitman Hooker Homestead in West Hartford, site of a colonial candlelight dinner and a birthday tea in honor of the first president.

Entertainment during the dinner includes taped readings of letters written to and from the Hooker Homestead, circa 1836. One letter from a sixteen-year-old girl tells of a trip she took from Hartford to Cincinnati via boat and rail. In another, a cousin bewails his difficulties in having a house built. He went on a business trip and returned to find that workmen had not done a thing while he was gone, which always causes guests to sigh, "What else is new?"

It's explained that in colonial times apple pie was considered a vegetable, not a dessert. So, at the colonial candlelight dinner your apple pie is served with the entree.

During Washington's birthday celebration, one can sample a tea typical of the Federal period which includes chicken or seafood sandwiches. Dessert usually consists of clove cake (a Washington family favorite) and a Hartford election cake, similar to a fruitcake and heavy on spices and either raisins or currants. It was served at gatherings of folks awaiting voting results when election day was a state holiday.

A latter-day tea, the Victorian Tea & Stroll, takes place in Collinsville, a town replete in Victorian architecture. After a guided walk through town, visitors are taken to the Canton Historical Museum, which has an abundance of Victorian memorabilia. It is at the museum where guests are served tea, scones, watercress or cucumber sandwiches, and small cakes.

Other Early American meals are served up with doses of history at venues such as the Mark Twain House in Hartford, and the Stanley-Whitman House and Hill-Stead Museum, both in Farmington.

FOR MORE INFORMATION

Contact: Farmington Valley Visitors Association, PO Box 1015, Simsbury, CT 06070; (800) 4-WELCOME (493-5266) or (860) 651-6950.

When in the area: On the campus of the University of Hartford in West Hartford is the Museum of American Political Life (Chapter 31).

Lodging: Executive Inn, 969 Hopmeadow Street (Route 10), Simsbury, CT; (860) 658-2216. Centennial Inn Suites, 5 Spring Lane, Farmington, CT; (800) 852-2052 or (860) 677-4647. The Farmington Inn, 827 Farmington Avenue, Farmington, CT; (800) 648-9804 or (860) 677-2821. Barney House (a 19th-century manor turned B and B), 11 Mountain Spring Road, Farmington, CT; (860) 674-2796. West Hartford Inn, 900 Farmington Avenue, West Hartford, CT; (860) 236-3221.

Early American Hearth Tours

42

Colonial Providence

TALK ABOUT GLOWING REVIEWS.

President John Quincy Adams once called it "the most magnificent and elegant private mansion that I have ever seen on this continent."

The abode in question is the John Brown House, built in 1786 on the corner of Benefit and Power streets in Providence. It is just one of many colonial vestiges of the Rhode Island capital waiting to be explored.

The John Brown in question here is not the abolitionist, but one of four brothers who endowed a school of higher education known in their time as the College of Rhode Island. The school then changed its name to give proper credit to the brothers with the cash and is known today as Brown University.

This particular member of the Brown family was one of the wealthiest citizens of Providence in his time, earning his fortune as a China trade merchant, slave trader, and privateer. Reminders of his years connected with his trade abound in the Georgian-style brick mansion. Vases, chairs, and screens, all of which have unmistakable oriental traits, dominate one upstairs bedroom, while the chamber named for John's wife, Sarah, is set up for an afternoon of tea; porcelain and other export ware make up the tea service.

As with all quality house tours, the guides here do not simply identify one artifact, then go on to the next. Instead, visitors learn about the social habits and behavior of colonial

New Englanders. In the formal downstairs parlor you learn that the pastimes of stylish adults included listening to live music (the only kind there was), singing, or playing blind-man's bluff in those days long before Monopoly and Trivial Pursuit. In the dining room you are handed a printed menu listing a likely dinner that would have been served in the season you are visiting.

Adams, as noted, may have paid the house the most elo-quent praise, but an eight-year-old boy named Alex gave it a more colloquial eulogy in 1987. He said, "Thank you for letting us go in the John Brown House. It was great. It was gigantic in there. I couldn't believe it. It was like the size of a brontosaurus."

Turn the corner onto Benefit Street to walk the "Mile of History" where there are historic houses the size of, maybe, pterodactyls. Most were built in the 18th and 19th centuries, and each tightly hugs its next-door neighbor.

The oldest is the Governor Stephen Hopkins House, at 15 Hopkins Street at the corner of Benefit. Hopkins was a signer of the Declaration of Independence, and his restored clap-board house dates from 1707. Poet Sarah Helen Whitman lived at 88 Benefit. At 75 North Main, near the corner of Ben-efit, is the First Baptist Meeting House, a classic colonial New England church with a towering steeple (185 feet high) and a Waterford crystal chandelier, crafted in 1792. The church was dedicated in 1775.

The Providence Athenaeum, at 251 Benefit, is a Greek Revival building dating from 1838 and is one of the oldest libraries in the country. At 224 Benefit is the Museum of Art of the Rhode Island School of Design, with works dating from ancient Rome and Greece to modern times.

The sidewalks on Benefit Street are made of brick, enhancing the thoroughfare's colonial flavor. The homes here are privately owned, although you do get to step inside some during the annual Festival of Historic Houses, spon-sored by the Providence Preservation Society and taking place in early June. Tickets are hot items.

Across Providence Harbor near City Hall is the Arcade, not a colonial site, but worth mentioning for those with cases of both history pneumonia and shopping pox. Dating to 1828, the Arcade is credited as the oldest indoor shopping mall in the country. It is a Greek Revival beauty with massive granite pillars at each end, facing both Weybosset and Westminster Streets. Hard to believe, but when built it sat in the middle of a cornfield.

Inside the Arcade are the types of stores and restaurants you would find at Boston's Faneuil Hall Marketplace or any of today's antique buildings-turned-shopping-malls. Expect to find everything from computer chips to chocolate chips.

Those still hungry for history may want to visit the Roger Williams National Memorial. It's a National Park Service site located at the exact spot where Roger Williams, the man found guilty in Massachusetts Bay Colony of "newe and dangerous opinions" such as religious freedom, established Providence in 1636. The site is a parklike setting and one of the few islands of green in downtown Providence.

A memorial at the site serves a dual purpose: marking the location of the freshwater spring used by Williams and his family and memorializing Judge Jacob Hahn, the first Jewish citizen elected to public office in the city, way back in the 1700s. Inside the visitor center are displays about the life and philosophies of Williams, a short video, and rotating exhibits on current issues; one such display focused on the local community of Jewish immigrants who settled in Providence after escaping religious persecution in Russia.

FOR MORE INFORMATION

Location: John Brown House is at 52 Power Street near the corner of Benefit Street. Governor Stephen Hopkins House is at the corner of Benefit and Hopkins Streets. The Arcade is at 65 Weybosset Street, downtown. Roger Williams National Memorial is at 282 North Main Street, on the east bank of the Providence River. Free parking for the national memorial is available in a lot on Canal Street behind the visitor center.

Admission: A fee is charged for the John Brown House; no charge for the Arcade and Roger Williams National Memorial.

Hours: John Brown House is open Tuesday through Saturday, and Sunday afternoon, March through December; Saturday all day and Sunday afternoon the rest of the year; closed holidays. The Arcade is open year-round, Monday through Saturday, also Sunday afternoon during the holiday season. Governor Stephen Hopkins House is open Wednesday and Saturday, afternoons only, and also by appointment in winter. Roger Williams National Memorial is open year-round, daily, except for Thanksgiving, Christmas, and New Year's Day.

Contact: John Brown House, 52 Power Street, Providence, RI 02906; (401) 331-8575. Providence Preservation Society (for Benefit Street information), 21 Meeting Street, Providence, RI 02903; (401) 831-7440. The Arcade, 65 Weybosset Street, Providence, RI 02903; (401) 456-5403. Roger Williams National Memorial, 282 North Main Street, Providence, RI 02903; (401) 521-7266.

When in the area: The Blackstone River Valley National Heritage Corridor is always pleasant to visit in fall (Chapter 32).

Lodging: Days Hotel on the Harbor, 220 India Street, Providence, RI; (401) 272-5577. Hi-Way Motor Inn, 1880 Hartford Avenue, Johnston, RI; (401) 351-7810. Ramada Inn/Providence-Seekonk, 960 Fall River Avenue, Seekonk, MA; (508) 336-7300. The State House Inn (a B and B built in 1890), 43 Jewett Street, Providence, RI; (401) 351-6111. Old Court Inn (a B and B built as a rectory in 1863), 144 Benefit Street, Providence, RI; (401) 751-2002.

43

Mystic Marinelife Aquarium

CROWDS IN MYSTIC MIGHT DISSIPATE IN WINTER, BUT THE aquarium's resident dolphins, Nina, Arrow and Misty, need not be lonely. The hordes are out of the way, and you have a greater opportunity to meet the amazing swimming mammals up close.

The dolphins and two beluga whales put on a regularly scheduled show, where they leap, speak (sort of), and exhibit other natural behavior in the aquarium's 1,200-seat marine theater. While you may have seen performance shows like this at other marine attractions, Mystic's aquarium permits one to view what goes on under as well as above the water.

Step down one flight directly below the theater and you are at the underwater level of the dolphin and whale tank. After the dolphins jump into the air, you are afforded a behind-the-scenes view (actually an "under-the-scenes" view), as they splash down with full force, rocketing under the water and then up again. The most amusing view might be the one of the dolphins' and belugas' bellies, while they float vertically with heads above the water and stomachs in your face.

Everyone has personal favorites here. Our four-year-old fell in love with the sea horses. She spotted them, then grabbed me and pulled me over to their tank. Having previously seen only pictures of sea horses in books, she said with glee, "I've never seen them real before." The sea horses put on a show by fluttering and flitting before us, with their minuscule featherlike appendages flapping back and forth.

And should you think penguins look like the caricatures in cigarette ads, plan a visit to the penguin pavilion. We learned that of the eighteen species of penguins in the world, only three live in the Antarctic. Those are the penguins of cartoons and advertising logos.

We saw one of the other fifteen species here. The African black-footed penguins residing in the aquarium live in temperate climates and are significantly smaller than Antarctic penguins, reaching a full height of only twenty-three inches.

Penguins don't fly, except as they speed through the water, where they swim up to twenty-five miles per hour. As with the dolphin and whale exhibits at the aquarium, the display is set up so that you can see the action both above and below the water. And we learned a fact that contradicts all those cartoons and advertisements that feature penguins and polar bears as buddies: Since all penguins live in the southern hemisphere, you will never see a penguin and polar bear together except on the drawing board in an office on Madison Avenue.

There is much more here relating to marine life. A hands-on exhibit permits one to control an undersea robot known as an ROV (remotely operated vehicle) and poke around a simulated shipwreck. New England coastal harbor seals and Alaskan sea lions alternately wobble on land and glide through water here. And you can stare eye to eye at a menacing shark, a ghostly, fat-faced skate, and dozens of varieties of other fish of every shape, size, and color.

Bear in mind that exhibits are both indoors and outdoors, so dress for the weather.

For More Information

Location: Mystic Marinelife Aquarium: From Interstate 95, exit 90, take Route 27 south, then take an almost immediate left onto Coogan Boulevard.

Admission: A fee is charged.

Hours: Year-round, daily, except for Thanksgiving, Christmas, and New Year's Day.

Contact: Mystic Marinelife Aquarium, 55 Coogan Boulevard, Mystic, CT 06355-1997; (203) 572-5955.

When in the area: Coastal Connecticut's maritime heritage is preserved at Mystic Seaport Museum, less than a mile down the road (Chapter 12).

Lodging: Best Western Sovereign Hotel—Mystic, 9 Whitehall Avenue, Mystic, CT; (860) 536-4281. Mystic Hilton, 20 Coogan Boulevard, Mystic, CT; (860) 572-0731. Comfort Inn of Mystic, 48 Whitehall Avenue, Mystic, CT; (860) 572-8531. Adams House (a 1790 home turned into a B and B), 382 Cow Hill Road, Mystic, CT; (860) 572-9551. Red Brook Inn (two colonial buildings turned into a B and B), 2750 Gold Star Highway, Mystic, CT; (860) 572-0349.

Mystic Marinelife Aquarium

44

Cross-Country Skiing

THE SETTING LOOKS LIKE A CHRISTMAS CARD COME TO LIFE: evergreens draped with snowy powder standing like sentinels of the woodlands. The feel is serene, gentle. Unsullied snow covers the ground. In the distance, a wisp of smoke curls from a chimney.

You're in the back woods of southern New England, gliding along groomed tracks or in the ungroomed wilderness of the states' forests and parks, with skis on your feet and the brisk air on your cheeks. You pause to savor the world of the cross-country skier, to listen to the soft sounds of winter, the flowing waters of a woodland brook, the trickle of snow melting off a maple branch in the sun.

In this hushed wilderness there are no major resorts like those you would find in Vermont's Green Mountains or in New Hampshire's White Mountains. Skiers here are enticed by what they see—well-kept 18th-century homes and miles and miles of woods, and by what they don't see—obtrusive crowds and cookie-cutter condominiums. You don't have to head north to find the New England you've always viewed on all those scenic calendars.

The major problem here is snow, or actually, the potential lack of it. Seaside towns warmed by ocean breezes are usually a no-show in the snow department. Rhode Island, practically engirded by sea water, is particularly vulnerable. Even inland, judging by the last several years, a dearth of snow is always possible. Then again, we can have a winter like that of 1995-96, with snow as high as the driver's seat of your next-door neighbor's Dodge Dakota. And when the snow is there, cross-country skiers are in for a thrill.

The sport has certainly grown over the last two decades. After all, it's cheaper than downhill and has been called by many the perfect aerobic sport, which is why there is a NordicTrak and not an AlpineTrak.

Rod Taylor, director of skiing and owner of the Woodbury Racquet and Ski Area in Woodbury, says that most skiers he sees are families or individuals dressed casually out for exercise and enjoyment. Still, he admits that the sport is getting very high tech, and there is a fair-size contingent of Nordic skiers dressed in Gortex and using specifically engineered equipment.

Taylor adds that the sport has also become more specialized, splintering into different styles such as telemarking (sort of a combination downhill/cross-country style) and skating style (exactly what it says it is) in addition to the traditional diagonal style. But, says Taylor, "Most want to go out and just have fun. You can cross-country ski any way you want, and many people find it hard to change their style."

Following are some of the top venues for cross-country skiing in Rhode Island and Connecticut.

Rhode Island

Casimir Pulaski Memorial State Park, Route 44 (mailing address: RR 2, Box 2185), Chepachet, RI 02814; (401) 568-2013. About four miles of groomed trails. Warming hut. A fee is charged.

Goddard Memorial State Park, Ives Road (off Route 1), Warwick, RI 02818; (401) 884-2010. Eighteen miles of ungroomed trails. No charge.

Norman Bird Sanctuary, 583 Third Beach Road, Middletown, RI 02842; (401) 846-2577. About three and a half miles of the sanctuary's property can be skied, along the Woodland, Main, and Quarry trails, all ungroomed. Visitor center available for warming up. A fee is charged.

Connecticut

Cedar Brook Cross Country Ski Area, 1481 Ratley Road (off Route 168), West Suffield, CT 06093; (860) 668-5026. 6.2 miles of trails, all groomed. Ski shop, snack bar. A fee is charged.

Mohawk Mountain Ski Area, 48 Great Meadow Road (off Route 4), Cornwall, CT 06753; (800) 895-5222 or (860) 672-6100. Five miles of ungroomed trails are in adjacent Mohawk Mountain State Park, not part of the private ski area. No charge. Ski area has ski shop and food service.

Pine Mountain Ski Touring Center, Route 179, East Hartland, CT 06027; (860) 653-4279. Fifteen miles of trails, all groomed. Light snacks in dairy barn on grounds. A fee is charged.

Weir Farm National Historic Site, 735 Nod Hill Road, Wilton, CT 06897; (203) 834-1896. A few miles of ungroomed trails are on the grounds. Cross-country skiers can also ski the roughly two and a half miles of ungroomed trails on the adjacent Weir Preserve of the Nature Conservancy. No charge.

White Memorial Foundation, 71 Whitehall Road (exit 42 off Route 8), Litchfield, CT 06759; (860) 567-0857. Thirty-five miles of ungroomed trails. No charge.

Winding Trails Cross Country Ski Center, 50 Winding Trails Drive (exit 39 off Interstate 84), Farmington, CT

Cross-Country Skiing

06032; (860) 678-9582. Twelve miles of groomed trails. Food. A fee is charged.

Woodbury Ski & Racquet Area, Route 47 (exit 15S or 17N off Interstate 84), Woodbury, CT 06798; (203) 263-2203. About twelve miles of trails, about 60 percent groomed and tracked. Two and a half kilometers (about one mile) is under lights and has snowmaking. Food and ski shop. A fee is charged.

Of Connecticut's fifty-one state parks, nearly half offer cross-country skiing. A total of seven of Connecticut's nine state forests have cross-country skiing. All state park and forest trails are free to use but are ungroomed. However, eleven have trail signs and maps. These include directional signs as well as those marking degrees of difficulty. Others have red "do not enter" slashes which are placed on hiking trails that are dangerous for skiing. They mean business.

State parks and forests offering cross-country skiing with signs are:

Bethel—Collis P. Huntington State Park, (203) 797-4165.

East Hampton—Hurd State Park, (860) 526-2336.

East Windsor—Flaherty Field Trial Area, (860) 684-3430.

Groton—Haley Farm State Park, (860) 445-1729.

Hamden—Sleeping Giant State Park, (203) 789-7498.

Hampton—James L. Goodwin State Forest, (860) 928-6121.

Hebron—Gay City State Park, (860) 295-9523.

Killingworth—Chatfield Hollow State Park, (860) 663-2030.

Litchfield—Topsmead State Forest, (203) 567-5694.

Mansfield—Mansfield Hollow State Park, (860) 928-6121.

Middlefield—Wadsworth Hall State Park, (203) 344-2950.

While the preceding parks and forests are the only ones for which signing and maps have been developed, nothing prevents any person from skiing on hiking trails in any state park or forest. Those with hiking trails but no signs or maps include:

Barkhamsted—American Legion State Forest and Peoples State Forest, (860) 379-2469.

Bloomfield—Penwood State Park, (860) 242-1158.

Colchester—Salmon River State Forest, (860) 295-9523.

Cornwall—Mohawk Mountain State Park, (800) 895-5222 or (860) 672-6100 (discussed under "Connecticut," preceding)

Derby—Osbornedale State Park, (203) 735-4311.

East Lyme—Rocky Neck State Park, (860) 739-5471.

Eastford—Natchaug State Forest, (860) 928-6121.

Groton—Bluff Point Coastal Reserve, (860) 445-1729.

Haddam—Cockaponset State Forest and Haddam Meadows State Park, (860) 345-8521.

Hamden/New Haven—West Rock Ridge State Park, (203) 789-7498.

Kent—Macedonia Brook State Park, (860) 927-3238.

New Fairfield—Squantz Pond State Park, (203) 797-4165.

Norfolk—Dennis Hill State Park, (860) 482-1817.

Oxford—Southford Falls State Park, (203) 264-5169.

Sharon—Housatonic Meadows State Park, (860) 927-3238.

Simsbury—Stratton Brook State Park, (860) 658-5593.

Torrington—Burr Pond State Park and John A. Minetto State Park, (860) 482-1817.

Voluntown—Pachaug State Forest, (860) 376-2920.

Watertown—Black Rock State Park, (860) 677-1819.

The best times to reach someone at the phone numbers listed are around 8 A.M. or between 3:30 and 4 P.M. At other times staff members are often out in the field. Keep in mind that the phone number is for the person responsible for the specific park or forest. It may not be physically at the same location.

Winter

FOR MORE INFORMATION

Contact: Bureau of Outdoor Recreation, Connecticut Department of Environmental Protection, 79 Elm Street, Hartford, CT 06106-5127; (860) 424-3200.

45

New England Air Museum

HELICOPTERS, PIPER CUBS, AND WORLD WAR II FIGHTER planes are roommates at the New England Air Museum at Bradley International Airport in Windsor Locks, Connecticut. Here, within an eye blink of New England's second busiest airport, is a massive collection of aircraft that affords visitors a hearty look at a full spectrum of aircraft technology.

The collection is housed in two buildings, one devoted mainly to military aircraft, the other to civil flying machines. As you might expect, there are several examples of Connecticut's contributions to the world of aviation. Consider Igor Sikorsky.

Born in Russia, Sikorsky left his homeland following the Bolshevik Revolution in 1917 and settled in Connecticut. In 1930 he shared predictions for the far-off year 1980 with the *New York Telegram*. A photocopy of the *Telegram* dated January 31, 1930, proves the man's sharp foresight. Sikorsky prophesied that there would be aircraft offering daily five-hour flights to Europe, that airplanes would achieve unheard-of speeds of 800 miles per hour, that "leviathans" would carry hundreds of passengers at one time, and that air travel would become routine and as safe as auto touring.

The floor is covered with Sikorsky helicopters as well as others by Kaman, Hiller, and Bell. The Sikorsky R-4B Hoverfly was a common sight during the Second World War, while the Bell OH-13E should induce visions of Hot Lips Houlihan and Corporal Klinger. This copter was best known for moving wounded servicemen from battle zones during the Korean War.

Then contrast the bulky helicopters with sleek fighters, like the Vought XF4U-4 Corsair with its unique inverted gull wings. The Corsair was the premier fighter used during World War II by both the navy and the marines. It was later used during the early stages of the Korean War.

Before names such as Pearl Harbor and Iwo Jima became household words—when the aircraft industry was still in its diapers—many entrepreneurs with mechanical skills dreamed of building a flying machine and starting their own businesses. One such person was a Connecticut machinist named Alexander Dydniuk.

From 1930 through 1934, Dydniuk developed and built his own airplane which he named the "Sport." It is reported that he flew in his airplane twice, performing loops and other gut-turning maneuvers for excited crowds. But any future for Dydniuk's "Sport" was dashed when the inventor was presented with necessary inspections, licensing requirements, and other regulations. Dydniuk dismantled the plane rather than deal with the drudgery of paperwork, and a potentially promising career was abated. The "Sport" is in the museum collection.

Nearby is the banana yellow 1937 Piper J-3 Cub, one of the most popular and enduring models ever produced. Its basic design was used as a prototype by many companies making larger planes over the last fifty years.

Long-time residents of the Windsor Locks area remember the date October 3, 1979, all too well. A deadly tornado, rare in these parts, had formed out of ominous dark clouds that had been hovering in the Connecticut sky. The tornado touched down on the museum grounds and went on a rampage. Aircraft that survived battles could not survive the day Mother Nature went berserk. Fighter planes were split in two as if they were paper gliders. Fifty-ton airplanes were

Winter

flipped over. Pieces of Plexiglas, aluminum, and fabric were found scattered across the tobacco fields of northern Connecticut.

Since then, the vast majority of the damaged planes have been repaired. The rest still show the twister's effects; it was not economically feasible or convenient to complete the repairs they needed.

Films on all aspects of aviation are shown regularly. Guided tours are by reservation only, but guides are on duty to answer your questions and share their expertise. Special events include lectures as well as Cockpit Tours, in which visitors can sit in the cockpits of several aircraft.

FOR MORE INFORMATION

Location: The New England Air Museum is next to Bradley International Airport. From Interstate 91, exit 40, follow the well-placed signs.

Admission: A fee is charged.

Hours: Year-round, daily, except Thanksgiving and Christmas.

Contact: New England Air Museum, Bradley International Airport, Windsor Locks, CT 06096; (860) 623-3305.

When in the area: To experience another way to travel, visit the Connecticut Trolley Museum (Chapter 20).

Lodging: Fairfield Inn by Marriott, 2 Loten Drive, Windsor Locks, CT; (860) 627-9333. Budgetel Inn, 64 Ella T. Grasso Turnpike, Windsor Locks, CT; (860) 623-3336. Holiday Inn–Bradley International Airport, 16 Ella T. Grasso Turnpike, Windsor Locks, CT; (860) 627-5171. Days Inn Bradley International Airport, 185 Ella T. Grasso Turnpike, Windsor Locks, CT; (860) 623-9417.

New England Air Museum

46

Getting into Yale

No need to travel to Manhattan to see the country's foremost museum collections. On the campus of Yale University in New Haven are some of the most highly regarded collections in America. And you don't have to take the SATs again to get in.

The dinosaurs on the ground floor of the Peabody Museum of Natural History fascinate all types from paleontologists to first-graders. "The Age of Reptiles," a 110′ ×16′ mural, dominates one gallery, with a stegosaurus, apatosaurus (the dinosaur formerly known as "brontosaurus"), and other monster lizards depicted in their natural habitats, chewing leaves or soaring through the air. Nearby is the humongous re-created skeleton of an apatosaurus. Known for what seems like an age as the brontosaurus, it was misnamed, experts now say.

The Yale University Art Gallery, a fixture since 1832, is the place to see works by Picasso, van Gogh, Gauguin, Rubens, Hopper, Homer, Pollock, and more. One must-see is van Gogh's *Night Cafe*, where downcast patrons bide time in an Arles, France, café. Another is the powerful *First Steps* by Picasso, capturing the tender moments of a child learning to walk. Calder's mobiles in the museum's Ordway Gallery attract modernists.

Noteworthy newly arrived modern works, both acquired by Yale in the 1990s, are *Stacks*, Richard Serra's rolled-steel sculpture; and Sol LeWitt's minimalist mural, *Untitled*, consisting of lines on a blue background drawn directly on the museum wall.

The university's other repository of art is the Yale Center for British Art, opened in 1977. The works of British artists such as John Constable, Thomas Gainsborough, William Hogarth, J. M. W. Turner, and George Stubbs are here.

You can also see *Nocturne in Blue and Silver*, completed in 1872 and 1878 by American expatriate artist James McNeill Whistler, who painted in London for years. The subject matter here is not Whistler's mother, but, said the *London Times* in 1878, "The Thames in a mist . . . a clocktower gleaming through the haze." It was in the hands of a Connecticut family for more than eighty years until purchased by the museum in 1995.

Thanks to a trio of brothers, Yale has one of the preeminent libraries of rare volumes. Edwin J., Frederick, and Walter Beinecke, who graduated from Yale in 1907, 1909, and 1910, respectively, were the major benefactors of the Beinecke Rare Book and Manuscript Library. The structure, with its dazzling six-story glass tower, was raised in 1963. Aside from the actual building, visitors will be intrigued by a couple of print originals: a Gutenberg Bible and two large folio volumes by American ornithologist and artist John James Audubon. They are displayed in the library's mezzanine gallery under glass. Pages are turned regularly to lessen exposure to light as well as offer different views.

The Yale University Collection of Musical Instruments also rates a note of interest. The elaborately painted spinets and harpsichords, adorned with likenesses of landscapes and allegorical scenes, are the most eye-pleasing displays. However, this museum is closed weekends.

General guided campus tours depart from the university visitor center at 149 Elm Street. They last about an hour and fifteen minutes and emphasize campus architecture and student life, taking visitors into the Beinecke Library, the Sterling Memorial Library (the main campus library), and two courtyards. You might also want to allow a few minutes to look around the visitor center, where a videotape is presented and historic photos are on view.

FOR MORE INFORMATION

Location: To reach the general campus area from Interstate 95, exit 3, head west on North Frontage Road, then north for three blocks onto York Street. The Peabody is a few blocks north of the main campus at the corner of Whitney Avenue and Sachem Street.

Admission: A fee is charged for the Peabody and the collection of musical instruments. Admission is free for the other museums and for guided campus tours.

Hours: The Peabody Museum of Natural History is open year-round, daily, and Sunday afternoon. Yale University Art Gallery is open September through July, Tuesday through Saturday, and Sunday afternoon. Yale Center for British Art is open year-round, Tuesday through Saturday, and Sunday afternoon.

Beinecke Rare Book and Manuscript Library is open year-round, Monday through Saturday; closed Saturday in August. Yale Collection of Musical Instruments is open September through June, Tuesday through Thursday, afternoons only. Guided campus tours are offered year round, twice daily weekdays and once daily on Saturday and Sunday.

Contact: Peabody Museum of Natural History, 170 Whitney Avenue, New Haven, CT 06520; (203) 432-5050. Yale University Art Gallery, 1111 Chapel Street, New Haven, CT 06520; (203) 432-0600. Yale Center for British Art, 1080 Chapel Street, New Haven, CT 06520; (203) 432-2800. Beinecke Rare Book and Manuscript Library, 121 Wall Street, New Haven, CT 06520; (203) 432-2977. Yale Collection of Musical Instruments, 15 Hillhouse Avenue, New Haven, CT 06520; (203) 432-0822. Yale University Visitor Center (for

Getting into Yale

guided campus tours), Box 201942, New Haven, CT 06520; (203) 432-2300.

When in the area: Urban treasures can be found in the often ignored city of Waterbury to the north (Chapter 36).

Lodging: The Colony (hotel within walking distance of campus), 1157 Chapel Street, New Haven, CT; (203) 776-1234. Holiday Inn at Yale, 30 Whalley Avenue, New Haven, CT; (203) 777-6221. Residence Inn by Marriott, 3 Long Wharf Drive, New Haven, CT; (203) 777-5337. Regal Inn, 1605 Whalley Avenue, New Haven, CT; (203) 389-9504. Econo Lodge, 7 Kimberly Avenue, West Haven, CT; (203) 932-8338.

Winter

47

Mark Twain and Harriet Beecher Stowe

Tom Sawyer and Huckleberry Finn, though remembered for their adventures on the Mississippi River, are natives of Hartford, Connecticut. Both boys were brought into this world in a rambling Victorian mansion, creations of the pen of Samuel Clemens, a.k.a. Mark Twain. It was while living in his Hartford home that Twain wrote his most famous works. In addition to *The Adventures of Tom Sawyer* and *The Adventures of Huckleberry Finn*, Twain authored *A Connecticut Yankee in King Arthur's Court* and *The Prince and the Pauper* while a Hartfordite.

Twain's next-door neighbor was a famed writer who fanned the flames of furor in the decade prior to the Civil War. Harriet Beecher Stowe published *Uncle Tom's Cabin* in 1852, and public reaction to her book has been credited for speeding the war's onset. Her home joins Twain's as tributes to two of the country's most illustrious authors.

From the street, the Twain home's maze of bay windows, gables, and turrets immediately strikes your eyes. But it is the dazzling Tiffany stained glass that makes visitors drool when they initially set foot in the 1874 mansion.

An antique telephone prompts the first insight to Twain's character and confirms his reputation as a cynic supreme. Twain grew to hate the newly invented device which he saw as an invasion of privacy and a source of interruptions. Your guide speaks of the time when, filled with holiday cheer, Twain wished a Merry Christmas and good will to all, "with the exception of the inventor of the telephone."

But you also discover a caring and sensitive Twain. In the library, a predecessor to today's family room, the author's children would beg him to tell impromptu stories incorporating statements about every piece of bric-a-brac decorating the mantel. Twain always complied with an exciting tale and never duplicated a previous story.

The library became the home's most public room, for guests as well as family. Twain's nephew, Jervis Langdon, wrote, "One of the pleasantest neighborhood customs that grew up in the Hartford home was the gathering, of an evening, around the library fire while Mr. Clemens reads aloud. He liked stirring poetry, which he read admirably, sometimes rousing his little audience to excitement and cheers."

But the dining room was also a center for entertainment, where Twain hosted such luminaries as Bret Harte, Matthew Arnold, and William Tecumseh Sherman. Twain loved to sit at the head of the table, facing a fireplace situated beneath an elongated window. In winter, he savored the view of snowflakes disappearing into the climbing flames.

What is almost every visitor's favorite chamber is the billiards room, which served double duty as Twain's workroom. It was here that he could often be found at both labor and leisure. After guests left, he would play billiards on his own through the wee hours. Twain's original billiards table is here. So are decorations of cues, pipes, and cigars that line the ceiling. His antiquated typewriter is emblematic of more serious activities; Twain was one of the first writers to type manuscripts.

Stowe's "cottage," a fourteen-room slightly Gothic house, appears to be of a different era from Twain's dark and heavy home. But despite the departure from typical Victoriana, this

Winter

house was built in 1871 and was planned to suit Stowe's tastes.

Stowe let sunlight literally brighten her day. Translucent curtains draped her windows, and in some cases she used plants to shield her windows instead. Her upstairs study is adorned with wallpaper filled with flowers and ferns, symbolic of her love of nature and gardening.

Although no records were kept of the appearance of her kitchen, the room has been furnished to the style set in *The American Women's Home*, a book written by Stowe and her sister Catharine in 1869.

Neatness is in command in the kitchen. The shelves are narrow, built specifically so that no item could be hidden behind another. Period kitchen pieces such as a soap cage, an eggbeater, and a pie holder all rest in proper places.

For More Information

Location: From Interstate 84, exit 46, turn right onto Sisson Avenue, then right onto Farmington Avenue to the homes.
Admission: A fee is charged for both homes.
Hours: The Mark Twain House is open Monday through Saturday, and Sunday afternoon, from Memorial Day through Columbus Day and in December; closed Tuesday the rest of the year; also closed Easter, Thanksgiving, December 24, Christmas Day, and New Year's Day; The Harriet Beecher Stowe House is open Monday through Saturday, and Sunday afternoon, June through Columbus Day; closed Monday the rest of the year; also closed Easter, Labor Day, Thanksgiving, December 24, Christmas Day, and New Year's Day.
Note: Although the houses sit side by side, they are operated by different organizations, which can be frustrating for visitors. For example, there is no combination discount ticket

for those wishing to see both houses. Also there are inconsistencies regarding hours—in the off-season the Stowe house is closed Monday, while the Twain house closes Tuesday.

Contact: Mark Twain House, 351 Farmington Avenue, Hartford, CT 06105; (860) 493-6411. Harriet Beecher Stowe House, 73 Forest Street, Hartford, CT 06105; (860) 525-9317.

When in the area: Hartford, founded in 1635 by Reverend Thomas Hooker, has a lengthy heritage and many historic places to explore (Chapter 7).

Lodging: Ramada Inn–Capitol Hill, 440 Asylum Street, Hartford, CT; (860) 246-6591. Super 8 Motel, 57 West Service Road, Hartford, CT; (860) 246-8888. Goodwin Hotel, 1 Haynes Street (across from the Civic Center), Hartford, CT; (800) 922-5006 or (860) 246-7500. The 1895 House B and B, 97 Girard Avenue, Hartford, CT; (860) 232-0014.

Winter

48

Christmas in Newport

A FESTIVAL OF FIRS, FEASTS, AND FANTASY IS CHRISTMAS AT Newport. The mansion halls are decked in their holiday finest, and the tastiest culinary repasts are served, giving all a chance to indulge in humankind's second-favorite vice. You can examine the myriad decorations on 100 trees and take part in a dinner with the famous Astors.

You won't mind that historical accuracy is stretched—the Vanderbilts, et al., were not in residence here in winter—and even if you don't know your Belmonts from your Astors, you won't care. The passion in Newport this time of year is not history, but fun.

The Preservation Society of Newport County, guardian of most of Newport's mansions year-round, open three every Christmas season. Depending on what year you visit, you might see Marble House, The Elms, Chateau Sur Mer, or The Breakers donning their holiday best. Chateau Sur Mer, dating from 1852, is usually decorated to fill the theme of A Victorian Christmas at Home, while The Elms, all pink and white, reflects the theme A French Noel.

The high point of a visit to Marble House is the ballroom's twenty-two-foot poinsettia tree, actually an intricate stacking of more than four hundred individual poinsettia plants. A tall tree dominates The Breakers as well. It reaches thirty-five-feet, is trimmed with red and silver balls, and stands in the Great Hall. Each mansion tour ends with a sampling of Christmas treats such as cookies and eggnog. And every Sunday one mansion is the setting for live music and a visit from Saint Nick handing out candy canes or otherwise greeting little ones.

Hungry for more sweets? Plan a Sunday visit to Belcourt Castle, a Gilded Age medieval-style chateau built by banker Oliver Belmont, and currently home to Donald Tinney and family. Christmas teas here last two hours and include a guided tour, a carol concert, and a gourmand's bounty of desserts. How do chocolate fudge torte, coconut chocolate chip cookies, hazelnut torte, and chocolate brownies sound for starters?

Belcourt Castle is open for tours at other times during Christmas at Newport. Visitors see an array of wreathes, silver balls, garlands, and Christmas trees, complementing original suits of armor and stained glass.

A full dinner is available at the Astors' Beechwood, where today's visitors join high society from the 1890s for a Christmas-season meal. Lasting more than two hours, this is a feast with entrees such as roast turkey with cranberry stuffing or braised leg of lamb in Reform Club sauce (a mix of red wine, red currant jelly, onions, ham, carrots, pecans, and varied herbs and spices first concocted at England's Reform Club during Queen Victoria's reign).

Entertainment comes in the form of carols and is provided by actors and actresses playing the Astors and their dignified guests. You will eat, drink, sing, and learn a bit about Victorian-era customs, too.

The Astors' Beechwood is also open for regular Christmas tours, which last about forty-five minutes and afford a view of one of the less ostentatious Newport mansions. The guides stay in character as Mrs. Astor's guests and employees, and offer a Christmas carol or two along the way.

There is also a wide range of events outside the mansions. The official opening is always December 1 in Washington Square, with the firing of cannons, a carol sing, a bonfire, and the obligatory cookies and cider. Another annual event is the Festival of Trees, each decorated differently. You will also find craft fairs, carol sings, and teas held by Newport churches and museums. Christmas in Newport always concludes with candlelight house tours of historic private homes for a few days after the presents have been opened and the eggnog drunk.

For More Information

Admission: A fee is charged for all Newport mansions, but admission is free to most special events.

Contact: Christmas in Newport, PO Box 716, Newport, RI 02840; (401) 849-6454.

Lodging: This is the B and B capital of southern New England. A partial list of Newport B and Bs includes: Cliffside Inn (former home of artist Beatrice Turner and repository for many of her works), 2 Seaview Avenue; (800) 845-1811 or (401) 847-1811. The Wayside, 406 Bellevue Avenue; (401) 847-0302. The Jailhouse Inn (a restored colonial jail), 13 Marlborough Street; (401) 847-4638. Brinley Victorian Inn, 23 Brinley Street; (800) 999-8523 or (401) 849-7645. The Willows, 8-10 Willow Street; (401) 846-5486.

There is also a B and B service listing rooms in more than 150 private homes, inns, and guest houses: Anna's Victorian Connection, 5 Fowler Avenue, Newport, RI 02840; (800) 884-4288 or (401) 849-2489.

Conventional motels in Newport include: Motel 6, 249 J. T. Connell Highway; (401) 848-0600. Best Western Mainstay Inn, 151 Admiral Kalbfus Road; (401) 849-9880. Newport Harbor Hotel & Marina, 49 America's Cup Avenue; (401) 847-9000.

49

Christmas Outside Newport

IT SEEMS AS IF NO ATTRACTION IN SOUTHERN NEW ENGLAND lets the holiday season slide by without dressing up in its holiday best. Consider the following:

Old Wethersfield, Connecticut In the historic corner of this Hartford suburb are some of the best-preserved colonial houses in the state. On one special day in December, there are demonstrations of dance, theatrical performances, and horse-drawn wagon rides down Main Street to the Captain James Francis House, fully decked in festive Victoriana.

Inside the Francis House, a three- to five-foot high Christmas tree is set on a table, as was the Victorian custom. Garnishing it are historically accurate paper ornaments and candles. Nearby are 19th-century toys, such as ring-toss games, dolls, and checkerboards. Close by, the Hurlbut-Dunham House is decorated for a 1930s Christmas, with a tree sprouting multicolored lights and glass ornaments. **Contact:** (860) 529-7656.

Christmas on Main Street Hartford, Connecticut. A Victorian Christmas tree sits atop a bundle of wrapped boxes in the Butler-McCook Homestead, a clapboard home built in 1782. The house, operated by the Antiquarian and Landmarks Society, is decorated to reflect a period when the McCooks lived here in the late 1800s.

Holidayfest and Bellamy-Ferriday House

Holidayfest and Bellamy-Ferriday House   Other holiday fests run by the Antiquarian and Landmarks Society include the aptly named Holidayfest, an arts-and-crafts display at the Hatheway House north of Hartford in Suffield. There is also an annual holiday exhibit at the colonial Bellamy-Ferriday House on Main Street in Bethlehem. The theme changes annually—one year there was a display of menorahs, from historic to modern to avant-garde.
Contact: (860) 247-8996.

Massacoh Plantation   Simsbury, Connecticut. "Three Centuries of Candlelight" is the name of the early-December living-history program at this multi-building complex. At an early-18th-century town meeting, a young woman may be accused of witchcraft, or the local free men might discuss where to build a new meeting house. In the Phelps House, scenes from the region's early-19th-century canal days are played out, while the Victorian-era Hendrick Cottage is host to an appearance by Saint Nicholas (as opposed to the 20th-century Santa Claus).
Contact: (860) 658-2500.

Gillette Castle   East Haddam, Connecticut. In the spacious living room of actor and playwright William Gillette's abode is a Christmas tree more than fifteen feet tall. Gillette's workshop is transformed into Santa's workshop with dummies of Santa and his elves hard at work. In Gillette's study there might be a tree graced with cat ornaments, in honor of the seventeen cats owned by Gillette (or, as any cat owner might say, who owned Gillette). Common holiday garnishes include poinsettias, garlands, and upwards of twenty wreaths hanging from the walls.
Contact: (860) 526-2336.

Mystic Seaport Mystic, Connecticut. Guided walks by the light of flickering lanterns take visitors back to Mystic, circa 1876. On the docks, wharf rats (homeless sailors) gather around a fire they built in a cauldron. In the stores, residents are doing last-minute shopping. Some folks in the tavern appear a bit too friendly. On board the ships, sailors in port celebrate a Christmas away from home.

There is one constant here: a century-old custom calls for Christmas trees to be placed atop ships' masts. Sailors once observed Christmas by decking their ships in that manner. A caveat: reserve a space on lantern tours as early as September if you can. They sell out quickly.
Contact: (860) 572-0711.

Christmas on the Trolleys At the Shoreline Trolley Museum in East Haven, the cars are decorated with tinsel and wreaths. Santa holds court in an antique trolley where he hands out cookies. The Connecticut Trolley Museum in East Windsor strings lights on brackets over the tracks. Take a ride and it appears as if you're rumbling through a multicolored tunnel. In the visitor center, Santa hands out candy canes.
Contact: Shoreline Trolley Museum, (203) 467-6927. Connecticut Trolley Museum, (860) 627-6540.

Blithewold Mansion and Gardens Bristol, Rhode Island. The forty-five-room mansion is dressed in its holiday best every December. The theme changes yearly, but there is always an eighteen-foot Christmas tree in the entrance hall. (Due to fire regulations, an artificial tree has replaced the natural trees once used here.)

Themes have included "Our Country Home," filled with greenery; 1920s Tiffany style with a heavy emphasis on silver and blue; and "Winter Wedding: A Romantic Christmas," with a bridal Christmas tree of silver and gold. Hot mulled cider is served.
Contact: (401) 253-2707.

Christmas Outside Newport

John Brown House   Providence, Rhode Island. The big day at this elegant late-Georgian-style abode is the holiday open house, always on a Sunday. There is live music, a children's storyteller, and free admission. At other times during the holiday season you can take a tour through the festive home, decked differently each year. One certainty is a display of toys dating from the 18th century to the present. **Contact:** (401) 331-8593.

A Celebration of Twelfth Night   Westerly, Rhode Island. An official goodbye to Christmas is the theme of this celebration on the weekend closest to January 6. The 200-voice Chorus of Westerly along with assorted court jesters, magicians, mimes, and jugglers make up this Renaissance-style program. Music can range from a rendering of the medieval "There is No Rose" to the customary "O, Come All Ye Faithful." In between the two performances is a peasant's feast, which one may attend separately or along with a show. Most peasants never ate like this; a recent entree was "Ye chicken embellished with mushroomes and sausage in the style of Twelfthe Night served wyth a fragrant sauce over Ye noodles." **Contact:** (401) 596-8663.

Winter

50

Snowshoeing

ROBERT FROST CALLED IT "THE ROAD NOT TAKEN."

One diehard said, "Snowshoers are individualists. They tend to go off on their own."

Snowshoeing has grown in popularity over the last two decades, but it never really became the trendy pastime that cross-country skiing did. It did not become the winter sport of the faddish. It has remained the sport of the self-determined person, the romantic, the loner, the individual who wishes to surround himself or herself with solitude.

Like the telephone, the snowshoe once came in one style: made of wood and laced with rawhide. Then came new technology. Aluminum replaced wood, and neoprene, a synthetic rubber, took the place of rawhide. Wood and rawhide snowshoes are still favored by the old-timers—hunters, ice fishermen, trappers, and the like—but the majority of weekend recreation-seekers favor synthetics. Nancy Waterhouse of the Wilderness Shop in Litchfield, Connecticut, concedes that she sells hardly any wooden snowshoes in her busy store.

Snowshoes have also gotten smaller and lighter, which means they are easier to maneuver. The most popular sizes are 8″ × 25″, 9″ × 30″, and 9″ × 34″. And more and more snowshoers are using ski poles for balance, just as more hikers are employing walking sticks. "You can get up and over things a little easier," says Waterhouse.

Why should one strap on a pair of snowshoes instead of skis? With snowshoes you can reach places skis can never reach, such as brush and twigs in the woods. You won't travel as fast on snowshoes as you will on skis, but if speed is your prime objective, choose another sport.

Snowshoes come in a wide range of styles. Bearpaws, pickerels, ojibwas, and beaver tails are not defunct USFL football teams. The bearpaw, or modified bearpaw, style of snowshoe is the most popular among recreational snowshoers. It is elliptical and has a rounded front end. Beaver tails are narrower, with pointed ends, and are favored by hunters; their shape makes them easily maneuverable in brush. Pickerels and ojibwas are popular with serious snowshoers out for long treks and with ice fishermen.

Expect to pay $10 to $15 to rent a pair for a day and between $125 and $275 to purchase a pair of shoes and bindings. It is highly recommended that newcomers to the sport rent a few times before investing in a pair.

Where are the best places in southern New England to follow Frost's "road not taken"? Just about any state park permits snowshoers, but head north for the better chances of finding the deepest snow. In Connecticut, Nancy Waterhouse likes White Memorial Foundation, (860) 567-0857, two miles west of Litchfield (off Route 202). The foundation has 4,000 acres of both flat, open areas and woods, and thirty-five miles of trails. Her other choice in the state's northwest corner is Mohawk State Forest, (860) 927-3238, outside Cornwall. The terrain there contains inclines and offers more challenges than flat terrain.

Joe Hickey, of Connecticut's Bureau of Parks and Forests, suggests a couple of state areas in the northeastern corner on opposite sides of Interstate 84 near Union: Bigelow Hollow State Park and Nipmuck State Forest, both (860) 928-9200. Both have fairly flat terrain on old forest roads and foot trails.

Winter

Many Rhode Island snowshoers admit that they leave the state for snowier climes. But if you wish to remain, check out Arcadia Management Area in Exeter, (401) 539-2356, the state's largest management area, measuring 14,000 acres. Its main access is on Midway Trail off Route 165. Native wildlife you might encounter include snowshoe hares (appropriately), white-tailed deer, mink, and foxes.

Paul Dolan, principal forester for the state, also suggests George Washington Management Area, (401) 568-2013, north of Route 44 in Glocester (five miles west of Chepachet Center). Snowshoers can cover the same gravel roads used by snowmobilers, although for safety reasons, cross-country trails are off-limits.

There's another safety advisory for Rhode Island snowshoers: Any time between October and February can be hunting season of some sort. Persons snowshoeing must wear 200 square inches of orange (about the size of a baseball cap) when in the wilderness during those months. (Although there is no such regulation in Connecticut, state wildlife department officials recommend that snowshoers wear brightly colored clothing during hunting seasons.)

Snowshoeing

FOR MORE INFORMATION

Contact: Connecticut Department of Parks and Recreation, (860) 424-3200. Rhode Island Department of Parks and Recreation, (401) 277-2632.

51

Rambling, Gambling Trips

IN CONNECTICUT, HOME TO BLUE BLOODS AND BLUE LAWS, gambling was once tsk-tsked as if it were blue movies. The closest that Connecticut folks could get to legal gambling was horse racing in Rhode Island. Some preferred to drive north to racetracks in Hinsdale, New Hampshire, and Pownal, Vermont.

Then in 1976 an import from Florida found its way up north. A greyhound racing track opened in Plainfield, Connecticut, near the Rhode Island border. Shortly afterwards, another import migrated our way; a jai alai fronton, for so long associated only with palm trees and piña coladas, became a vision on the landscape bordering Interstate 91 in Hartford.

Around that time, Native Americans began realizing the money to be made from legalized gaming. Bingo centers began appearing on Indian land in the West. In the East, the Mashantucket Pequots opened Foxwoods Resort Casino near Ledyard, Connecticut, in 1992. In October 1996, the Mohegans flung open the doors on their own Mohegan Sun Casino in Uncasville, Connecticut, just ten miles away.

Meanwhile, in Lincoln, Rhode Island, they are still off and running at Lincoln Park, although today the four-legged racers are greyhounds, not Thoroughbreds. And there are now at Lincoln the additional diversions of simulcasts and video slot machines.

The Hartford jai alai fronton is gone, but pelotas fly in Milford, Connecticut. Close by in Bridgeport, greyhounds race, and in Newport, Rhode Island, land of the Astors and Vanderbilts, there is another jai alai fronton.

So, now we have a bit of Las Vegas in southern New England, but without the erupting street volcanoes or floor shows with titles like "Nudes on Ice." And there is no question that a gambling market exists.

On October 12, 1996, when Mohegan Sun Casino first opened its doors, 150 cars were lined up on the access road to the casino at 4 a.m. The casino wouldn't officially open until six hours later. By noon the parking lots were filled nearly to capacity, and there were 15,000 to 18,000 pleasure seekers inside.

Two of the world's three largest casinos are Foxwoods (the largest) and Mohegan Sun (third-largest). (The second-largest is the MGM Grand in Las Vegas.) Foxwoods has two large casino rooms, a large slot parlor, a bingo room, a keno lounge, a smorgasbord of restaurants, and a theater called Cinetropolis, where seats with six-direction motion move in sync with the action on the screen. The number of slot machines totals more than 4,300, and there are 300 gaming tables. A state-of-the-art museum chronicling the lengthy history of the Mashantucket Pequot tribe opened in 1998.

Mohegan Sun is arranged in a circular design and is divided into four sectors with four entrances, representing the four winds and underlining the importance of seasonal changes to Mohegan life. Inside are about 3,000 slot machines, 180 gaming tables, a bingo hall, several restaurants, and an entertainment complex for kids.

Two facets of gambling you won't find at the casinos are jai alai and racing. For the uninitiated, jai alai (to regulars, it's "hi-li") is a bit like a combination of tennis and handball, except that the ball (or pelota) is caught in, then released from, a long, curved wicker basket called a cesta. As in handball, there is no net. If you were around in the Basque region of northern Spain 400 years ago, you could have seen jai alai matches played against church walls. In southern New England you will find them in arenas (called frontons) in Newport and Milford. Unlike most other betting games, you wager your money on the performances of humans.

Bob Heussler of Milford Jai-Alai recommends for novices, "It's a good idea to watch a game or two before you bet, for orientation, but directions (for the game) are printed in the program. Play-offs can be confusing, but always ask any questions to the ushers or other staff."

There are no other gaming pursuits at Milford Jai-Alai, but Newport Jai-Alai has horse-racing simulcasts and about 400 video slot machines. These slots do not have the outrageous payoffs you will find in major casinos, but most of us would be happy with a maximum jackpot of $6,000. Of course, more players lose than win, but if you are fearful of losing your shirt, listen to the advice of Paul Kasparson of Newport Grand Jai-Alai.

Kasparson suggests, "If you don't go bonkers, you can have a nice evening out for the same cost of an evening at a nightclub in Boston. Have dinner and drinks, put about $20 in the slots, and bet each jai alai meet."

There is no longer horse racing in southern New England, but the three greyhound tracks offer chances to gamble on the animals. Lincoln Park has the largest array of features. In addition to live greyhound racing, Lincoln boasts simulcast Thoroughbred racing and 1,200 video slot machines (maximum jackpot total of $6,000). Shoreline Star Greyhound Park and Entertainment Complex in Bridgeport and Plainfield Greyhound Park both feature live racing and simulcasts, but no slots.

Shoreline Star's general manager, Steve Alford, comments that weekdays and weekends draw two distinct crowds. "On Wednesday and Thursday we get the diehard gamblers," Alford notes. "On Saturday and Sunday it's a more casual crowd. On Saturday evening we get many people

Rambling, Gambling Trips

from New York or New Jersey who want to have a nice dinner and spend a little money. Some come to just watch the races and not bet much, or not bet at all, although that's just a small number."

Alford adds that a program, sold at a nominal charge, is a big help for novices and "is quite a bit simpler than a horse-racing form, which can be intimidating, even for me."

FOR MORE INFORMATION

Admission: A fee is charged for Milford Jai-Alai; admission is free for the other complexes.

Hours: Newport Grand Jai-Alai has live meets roughly May through October and offers simulcasts year-round. Milford Jai-Alai and the greyhound tracks offer live meets or races year-round. The casinos are open year-round. Open days for the tracks and frontons often change. Call ahead before making a special trip to either jai alai fronton or any greyhound track.

Contact:

Mashantucket Pequot Tribal Nation Foxwoods Resort Casino, (800) FOXWOOD (369-9663) or (860) 885-3000.

Mohegan Sun Casino, (888) 226-7711 or (860) 848-5682.

Newport Grand Jai-Alai, (800) 451-2500 or (401) 849-5000.

Milford Jai-Alai, (800) 243-9660 or (203) 877-4211.

Lincoln Park, (401) 723-3200.

Plainfield Greyhound Park, (800) 722-3766 or (860) 564-3391.

Shoreline Star Greyhound Park and Entertainment Complex, (800) 972-9471 (Connecticut), (800) 243-9490 (New York and New Jersey), or (203) 576-1976.

52

Happy New Year!

WHAT IS IT THAT TURNED FIRST NIGHT, A YEAR-END celebration in the city of Boston in 1976, into a North American phenomenon? As we went to press, there were 165 First Night festivities ringing in the year across the United States and Canada, from Boston to Honolulu, from Saint John, New Brunswick, to Victoria, British Columbia.

We went straight to the horse's mouth and spoke to Zeren Earls, one of the creators of the first First Night and currently president of First Night International, an umbrella group overseeing all First Night celebrations.

According to Earls, "By the 1970s, New Year's Eve had become an empty holiday. You either stayed home and watched the ball drop or spent a lot of money and went out and maybe had not that good of a time. We wanted to offer an alternative."

Rita Smircich, an organizer of First Night Westport/Weston in Connecticut, seconds those sentiments. She says, "New Year's Eve had become a holiday for couples. First Nights are for everyone. You can come with a group of people or on a date or with your family."

But Earls brings up another reason she suspects why people are flocking back downtown to watch live entertainment and . . . God forbid . . . interact with other human beings.

"We spend all our days in front of screens," observes Earls. "We go from sitting in front of a computer screen at work in the day to sitting in front of a TV screen at home at night. We are losing our sense of community, of our cities. First Night makes a difference, at least at this one time of year."

The debut First Night in southern New England was in Providence on December 31, 1984. Today there are seven First Nights in Connecticut and Rhode Island. All are similar in many ways, but there are subtle differences.

In general, First Nights begin early in the afternoon on December 31 and last until a little past midnight. Afternoon activities are heavy on kid stuff. Little ones can hear live music or make crafts such as noisemakers or funny hats. There might be a children's masquerade or a parade with giant puppets.

After the dinner hour, the entertainment becomes less child oriented, which is not to say it becomes adult oriented. You might hear the smoky strains of Dixieland jazz as opposed to Raffi-type sing-alongs. Instead of clowns, stand-up comedians may provide the laughs, but the only four letter word you will perhaps hear is "snow." And most end with a fireworks show at midnight.

Alcohol-free is a cardinal rule of all First Nights. A First Night might be a mass gathering of people, but it is no Mardi Gras. There are no naked people on the streets, but no beaten ones, either. Crime is a rarity during First Nights.

Following is a list of the current First Nights in Connecticut and Rhode Island:

First Night Providence   Rhode Island, since December 31, 1984. The convention centers and performing-arts centers are the venues for the visual artists. Children, meanwhile, can make masks, wind streamers, noisemakers, or hats at Imagination Market and show them off at the Children's Procession in the evening. Draws about 55,000. (401) 521-1166.

First Night Hartford   Connecticut, since December 31, 1989. There is a heavy accent on world music, and two fireworks shows: one at 6 P.M. for youngsters to enjoy, and another at midnight. Just before midnight, a procession begins at city hall and ends at Bushnell Park. Draws about 30,000. (860) 728-3089.

First Night Danbury   Connecticut, since December 31, 1989. A wide range of music is heard, including reggae, folk, big band, Caribbean, and country. There are no fireworks, but the event once ended with the falling of a huge lit hat, similar to Times Square's ball. (Remember that Danbury was known as the Hat City.) Draws about 10,000. (203) 792-5095.

First Night Norwalk   Connecticut, since December 31, 1994. Afternoon events are held downtown, where kids with freshly painted faces can march in a parade. Evening happenings are centered around trendy SoNo (South Norwalk), less than a mile away. Singers, dancers, and stand-up comedians from the local Tree House Comedy Club perform. Draws about 3,000 to 5,000. (203) 838-9444.

First Night Westport/Weston   Connecticut, since December 31, 1994. This First Night prides itself on its professional performers, most of whom reside in Fairfield County. Each year there is a theme. At the "International" First Night, one could hear anything from Klezmer to Brazilian tunes. At "Americana" First Night, it was bluegrass and Native American music. Draws about 6,000 to 7,000. (203) 454-6699.

First Night, Mystic   Connecticut, since December 31, 1994. Staff members call this celebration one of the more intimate First Nights, with all events held in and around a small area on Main Street. Fireworks light the sky over the Mystic River, and replica trolleys are pulled by horses. Supplementing the music is an annual performance by popular

Happy New Year!

hypnotist Jim Spinnato. Limited to 5,500 people. (860) 536-3575.

Opening Night, Newport   Rhode Island, since December 31, 1993. Though not an official First Night celebration, this event celebrates the arts just the same. One difference here is that festivities end with fireworks at 9 P.M., not at midnight. A staffer explains that the occasion is heavy on children's programming, and most parents do not want young ones up until midnight, regardless of the holiday. Draws 3,000 to 5,000. (800) 326-6030 or (401) 849-8048.

First Night, Westerly   Rhode Island, since December 31, 1995. During the day, kids can walk through a life-size maze or admire some 2,000 luminaria in Wilcox Park. Thanks to friends in high places, organizers were able to persuade Nickelodeon Television Network to offer one of their popular slime shows at the local YMCA. At night people gather to watch a lit ball dropping down the flagpole at the post office. Draws about 6,000 to 7,000. (401) 596-7761.

Winter

Index